The Jagged Journey

THE JAGGED JOURNEY

Suffering—God's Heart and Our Calling

Barry L. Callen

CASCADE Books • Eugene, Oregon

THE JAGGED JOURNEY
Suffering—God's Heart and Our Calling

Copyright © 2018 Barry L. Callen. All rights reserved. Except for brief quotations in critical publications or reviews, no part of this book may be reproduced in any manner without prior written permission from the publisher. Write: Permissions, Wipf and Stock Publishers, 199 W. 8th Ave., Suite 3, Eugene, OR 97401.

Cascade Books
An Imprint of Wipf and Stock Publishers
199 W. 8th Ave., Suite 3
Eugene, OR 97401

www.wipfandstock.com

PAPERBACK ISBN: 978-1-5326-3973-9
HARDCOVER ISBN: 978-1-5326-3974-6
EBOOK ISBN: 978-1-5326-3975-3

Cataloguing-in-Publication data:

Names: Callen, Barry L., author.

Title: The jagged journey : suffering—God's heart and our calling / Barry L. Callen.

Description: Eugene, OR: Cascade Books, 2018 | Includes bibliographical references.

Identifiers: ISBN 978-1-5326-3973-9 (paperback) | ISBN 978-1-5326-3974-6 (hardcover) | ISBN 978-1-5326-3975-3 (ebook)

Subjects: LCSH: Suffering—Religious aspects—Christianity.

Classification: BT732.7 .C335 2018 (print) | BT732.7 (ebook)

Manufactured in the U.S.A.   05/11/18

Dedication

I am a man blessed with wonderful grandchildren, the best. They are the future. I dedicate this work to them, hoping that each will come to know two key things:

- The loving and self-giving heart of God;
- The compassionate life to which God's children are called.

As they travel what at times likely will be a jagged journey of faith, may they embrace and rejoice in this great news and big challenge—

> Your life is a journey you must travel with a deep consciousness of God. It cost God plenty to get you out of a dead-end, empty-headed life. He paid with Christ's sacred blood, you know. . . . If we walk in the light, God himself being the light, we experience a shared life with one another as the sacrificed blood of Jesus, God's Son, purges all our sin.
>
> — 1 Peter 1:18, 1 John 1:7, The Message

PATH OF THE JAGGED JOURNEY

Foreword | ix

SOME BASICS

1. Opening Confessions: *We Wish It Were Otherwise, But It Isn't!* | 3
2. Biblical Signposts: *The Bible Gives Us Both Mixed Messages and Sure Anchors* | 15
3. The Path Ahead: *God Will Show the Way Even When There Appears to Be No Way* | 34

WE SAY:

Take it Away! (2 Cor 12:8)

4. Burden of the Mystery: *With Things This Way, Can God Really Exist?* | 47
5. God and Evil: *Isn't Evil and Injustice God's Own Fault?* | 56
6. Even Jesus Cried: *Can God Suffer and Still Be God?* | 65

GOD SAYS:

My Grace is Sufficient! (2 Cor 12:9)

7. Shock 'n Awe: *But, God, I Didn't Do It! This Isn't Fair!* | 79

8. Doubt Your Doubts: *Any Chance that Our Doubts Themselves Deserve Doubting?* | 88

9. Night Stars: *The Darker the Night the Brighter the Stars* | 97

10. Managing the Journey: *How Can I Find Pleasure in Pain?* | 106

THE FACT IS:
Weakness Can Be Strength (2 Cor 12:10)

11. Training for Christ-likeness: *Shortcuts Are Not Allowed* | 121

12. Thorns Changed to Crowns: *There Is a Way for the Worst to Become the Best!* | 134

13. God with Us Always: *If Only Someone Were by My Side!* | 145

Notes | 158

FOREWORD

Robert Kennedy rose to make a campaign speech to an enthusiastic crowd near my home in Indiana. It was a fateful day in 1968. Instead of his prepared speech, he quieted the crowd and dramatically changed the subject, announcing the assassination that very day of Martin Luther King, Jr. Kennedy, soon to be gunned down himself, proceeded to deliver a somber speech urging calm, love, and peacefulness in honor of the slain prophet of non-violent social change. Kennedy's words of calming wisdom included these:

> My favorite poet is Aeschylus. He once wrote, "And even in our sleep, pain which cannot forget falls drop by drop upon the heart until, in our own despair, against our will, comes wisdom through the awful grace of God."

This present book echoes the sentiment of these ancient poetic lines. In the journey of faith in this broken world, the follower of Jesus Christ will encounter a jaggedness that can injure and confuse. There will be instances of pain, injustice, violence, and grief. But there also will be bursts of love and glimpses of wisdom and hope coming through the sheer grace of God.

SOME BASICS

1

OPENING CONFESSIONS

We Wish It Were Otherwise, But It Isn't!

A mortal, born of woman, few of days and full of trouble, comes up like a flower and withers, flees like a shadow and does not last. . . . Don't blame fate when things go wrong—trouble doesn't come from nowhere. It's human! Mortals are born and breed for trouble as certainly as sparks fly upward.

Job 14:1-2; 5:7

Life is pain, Highness. Anyone who says differently is selling something.

The Princess Bride (1987)

This is a book I would have chosen not to write, but somehow there was no choice. It's an unavoidable subject, God and human suffering. What a difficult and troubling combination of words! For those who believe in an all-powerful God, the suffering of anyone, and especially of those who love and serve God, is troubling. Even more troubling is the thought that God suffers because we sin.

A best seller was Rabbi Harold Kushner's book *When Bad Things Happen To Good People*.[1] Why should that ever happen to good people? And how could it possibly be that God suffers when we do? Well, biblical revelation makes clear that suffering resides at the center of God's heart and also is key to our calling as followers of Jesus. Anyone who tells you differently is selling something.

Does God *Cause* or Just *Help* Our Suffering?

I confess. Like Harold Kushner, I don't want to treat suffering like a crossword puzzle, making every piece fit together neatly and thus not reaching people where they are—hurting! Suffering people want an answer to the question, "Why?" They don't want a graduate class in technical theology. But what if any satisfying and responsible answer to the "Why?" question requires clarifying some basic theological assumptions? Sorry, but it does. That's what chapters two and three of this book are about.

Those suffering often tend to assume that God controls everything and must have a reason for having brought the suffering. Presumably God caused it, or at least allowed it because of what the sufferer did to deserve it. So the questions come. Did I do something wrong or does God have reasons beyond my comprehension? Either way, the answer leaves sufferers hating themselves for being at fault or feeling badly toward God who brought the pain, won't explain why, and makes things worse by not stopping it.

> Suffering haunts all humans sooner or later. When it does, it raises difficult questions, even for a devoted Christian.

There's got to be a better answer to "Why?" than "we all get what we deserve." Our experience tells us that many people don't get what they deserve, despite Isaiah 3:10–11 and Proverbs 12:21. This world isn't as neat a place as Psalm 92:6–8, 13, 16 describes. Therefore, we're left with pushing off until the judgment of eternity the straightening out of all the earthly injustices. Or we come to another insight that frees us to think again. Maybe the Bible reports our many human thoughts on the matter of suffering but doesn't necessarily *teach* as truth all that it *reports*.

If Psalm 92 is too neat a picture of the world we know—the righteous, in fact, don't always flourish like a palm tree, then Psalm 121 might help. It says that relief from our suffering comes from the Lord. This implies that our *help* and not necessarily our *suffering* comes from God. We must be careful what we decide to lay at the feet of God.

Suffering haunts all humans sooner or later. When it does, it raises the most difficult of questions, even for the devoted Christian. We cry in pain and reach out in desperation and confusion. We believe, and then we're not sure we can believe. We want healing and death comes. The best we can say then is that death is the ultimate healing. Yes, in a sense it is, but why the substantial suffering on the way?

It's Always with Us

Recent history has made doubting very tempting. The twentieth century witnessed two world wars, the Holocaust, and the dropping of two atomic bombs with the development of much more terrible ones we're now so afraid may be used at any time. Ours is the age of Auschwitz and Hiroshima. There have been recent genocides in the Soviet Union, China, and Rwanda, devastating famines in Africa, the killing fields of Cambodia, the emergence of the AIDS pandemic, and the ethnic cleansing of Kosovo. That's just a partial list.

And the twenty-first century hasn't started any better. There already have been 9/11 in the United States, unspeakable horrors in Syria, thousands dying in the attempt to cross the Mediterranean to reach Europe, cancer and divorce becoming so common, and on and on. Will my grandchildren have to endure a nuclear winter? The blockbuster movies are full of the most shocking images of what might soon be. Jesus said we always would have suffering in this world (John 16:33). We sure do!

My friend Phil Meadows addressed the Wesleyan Theological Society in 2017 from his vantage point of today's British Isles—although the trend is the same across Europe and in the United States. Governments, he said, are trying to stop "radicalization" that leads to violence. While understandable, and likely those nervous governments are aiming mostly at Muslims, it's a new challenge to be a serious Christian in a post-Christendom society. It threatens anyone who believes that obedience belongs to the kingdom of God before the "rule of law" in any modern country. Protesting this secularizing and nation-protecting trend that could soon target Christians in England, Meadows reported that the Archbishop of Canterbury announced that he was a religious "extremist"!

Being persecuted for holding the "dangerous" position that the state is not ultimate is an old problem. Meadows noted that Methodism in eighteenth-century England was little understood and easily suspected of being unpatriotic. He insisted that authentic discipleship will give "continual offence" that leads to persecution. Even so, the true follower of Jesus must "pursue a life of radical discipleship in a world of unbelief."[2] Might your church be the next target of government? If you will recall, that's basically why Jesus was murdered!

Injustice at the hands of powerful non-church leaders is an evil that often haunts the faithful. Why doesn't God stop it? Why did God cause or at least allow his own Son to die? If God really is almighty, how can suffering persist and God be good? It's a question so basic that it can't be avoided, and there's no quick and easy answer. Don't look for a simplistic one in these pages. That's my first confession, my limited ability to solve a subject of such massive dimensions with some superior reasoning that only I have. Even so, I can't ignore it, nor can you, and there's much to be gained from addressing this hard subject aggressively—although not arrogantly.

The chapters of this book will follow what Paul pictures in 2 Corinthians 12 as the usual path taken by the Christian sufferer—from "maybe God can't even be" to "God is always with us, even in our pain." Getting from the beginning to the end of this precarious path can be—will be—a *jagged journey*. The Bible is full of testimonies and helpful trail-markers, to be sure, and I will point them out in chapter two. I also will identify biblical signposts, mixed messages, and at least a few sure truth anchors.

Since our world and our personal lives are full of tragic happenings, we long for any help we can find and trust. But we must be careful not to make the bottom line the first Bible verse we come to. There are many of them and they don't all seem to point in the same direction. I'll do my best to be a dependable guide.

Grabbing at Answers

Here's another confession. I confess some bewilderment at all the questions, as do most people who are suffering. Why is this world so full of pain? Why do Christians fall ill? We are betrayed. We go broke. A child goes astray. We're told by a doctor that the tests show that we're dying. Another war breaks out and demands our young as grist for its relentless mill. Maybe in your case the pain is something smaller, private, trivial, but still truly annoying. A little book of devotions for high school students is titled *If God Loves Me, Why Can't I Get My Locker Open?* Events may seem small and even amusing to others, but faith can be pulled apart by them.

Is God really with us? Why don't things go more smoothly? Does our faith get buried with our bones? Does God even exist? Is new life really waiting around the corner, or am I just kidding myself? It's easy to be quite unsure when we're hurting, frustrated, lost. And that's much of the time for many who find themselves grabbing for answers.

How does hurting relate to being *holy*? Are there real answers to the pressing questions raised by suffering? Shouldn't believing put some wall of protection around us? Does suffering defy apparent reason if God supposedly is good and all-powerful? Is our faith being mocked just when we need it most? Isn't God's reputation suffering when those dedicated to the divine are bleeding, grieving, persecuted, and dying despite their faith?

We believe sincerely and hurt anyway. Why? Does the persecution of God's saints cancel the high claims of God's dearest children? Does pain prove that God either *is not* or *cannot*? On the other hand, can pain bring new possibilities? Does true faith in Jesus bring with it the ability to use suffering for good? Can we flourish despite suffering? Is there any end to these questions?

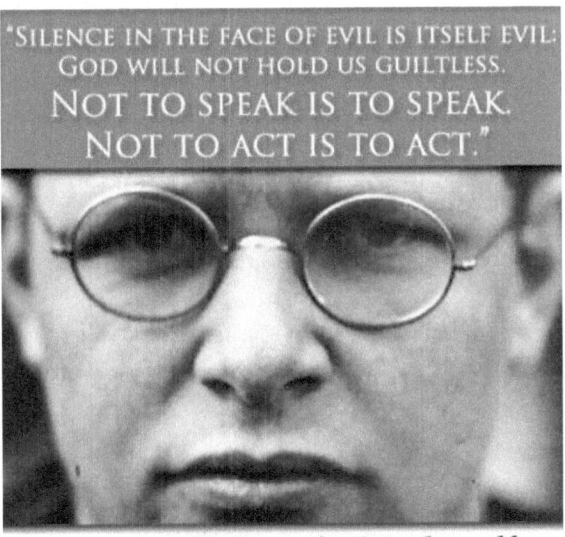

"Silence in the face of evil is itself evil: God will not hold us guiltless. Not to speak is to speak. Not to act is to act."
- Dietrich Bonhoeffer

Wisdom is found in these words, although it's hardly welcome: "The Son of God suffered unto the death, not that men might not suffer, but that their sufferings might be like His."[3] While this is right according to orthodox Christianity, being right doesn't settle everything. I want my faith to shield me from suffering and not lead me into it like it did Christ.

Can it really be that God suffers and gives us the "privilege" of joining in the divine misery? We hope not. Who wants to suffer unto death and do it voluntarily? Can we worship a God who also is caught in suffering? Doesn't God's "sovereignty" trump the possibility of divine suffering? These are hard questions that haunt our fragile faith. Looking the other way and believing blindly surely isn't the answer. Hard questions are there and must be faced.

Does God suffer, even to the point of death? How can God suffer, even die, and still be God? If God has done whatever is necessary to address the problem of our suffering, why must we still suffer, and how can we feel privileged to do so? Is God's healing arm too short to reach us? If we believers are now called to endure pain like Jesus, what's the nature and purpose of his suffering that we must share? If we can't avoid it, can we bear it?

The questions fly at us, and sometimes bits of answers also sail by and are grabbed quickly or they're gone. For instance, this flew by me once. William Faulkner was asked how he went about writing a book. His answer: "It's like building a chicken coop in a high wind. You grab any board or shingle flying by or loose on the ground and nail it down fast." That's exactly how I've had to do things over the years. I've written books while busy about other responsibilities, grabbing quiet minutes and nailing down thoughts that were flying by me.

And that's how it worked with this book on suffering. There was a word someone spoke, a line I happened to read, and a momentary inspiration surely from God. I grabbed, then nailed it down, and finally polished and published. I heartily subscribe to this wisdom of Eugene Peterson: "Time, but not just time in general, abstracted to a geometric grid on a calendar or numbers on a clock face, but what the Greeks named *kairos*, pregnancy time, *being present to the Presence*. I never know what is coming next; 'Watch therefore.'"[4]

Of all subjects, suffering demands being very present to the Presence, kneeling before the throne of God. If the sufferer will just "watch therefore," sometimes it just happens. God is there. An insight sustains. Strength comes. Despite everything, life wins!

What Do I Know?

I have yet another confession. I haven't learned all there is to know about suffering with and for Jesus. Yes, I've had cancer and lost a wife to cancer. Yes, I've had all of the childhood diseases and the usual complaints of growing older. I once was told that I was on the hit list of a foreign despot in Africa because of a Christian ministry in which I am involved there. An academic program in which I was enrolled in the turbulent 1960s required that I survive on the streets of Chicago for five days with only five dollars in my pocket.[5] But I've been healthy and safe for the most part, and privileged to live in a prosperous country free of any severe persecution for my faith.

Why, then, am I qualified to write about suffering, holiness, the nature of God, and victory over suffering? It's because I've delved deeply into biblical revelation and found some answers. What wisdom I have comes somewhat from personal experience, somewhat from the testimonies of a few wonderful saints of God I've known well, but mostly from the gracious gifting of the self-revealing and voluntarily suffering God who speaks through the Bible. I take no credit for what I share, but rejoice that I have something truly important to report.

Here's a further word about the Bible as my key source. Suffering is one of the Bible's main themes, maybe its largest theme. It begins with an account of how evil and death came into the world. The major Exodus story recounts Israel's forty years of intense trials in the wilderness after the terrible slavery experienced in Egypt. The Exile is the story of a deep shadow cast over a large portion of the journey of God's people. Exodus-Exile loom over the whole Old Testament. In addition, the Wisdom literature is largely dedicated to the problem of suffering. Ecclesiastes ponders the perplexing questions of evil and our human mortality. Job cries out. The Psalms sing out, often in pain.

There's no end to this biblical recounting and grabbing for help in the face of suffering. The New Testament books of Hebrews and 1 Peter are almost entirely devoted to helping people face relentless sorrows and troubles, while Revelation screams of persecution faced by God's faithful people across the ages. Towering over all, of course, is the Bible's central figure, Jesus Christ, who comes to us as a man of sorrows crucified for the sins of the world. The biblical writers knew the depths of the human experience and point to the possible heights of the way through it. See chapter two for some key biblical signposts and truth anchors.

How I Got Started

Being steeped in biblical revelation was clearly one reason I began exploring and writing about the jagged faith journey through suffering. Another reason was having a wife and then two dear friends die after years of battling cancer, while two more were still in the fight and my sister almost lost her battle. Then came my reading of a series of sermons on suffering by one of the Scottish greats, James Stewart.[6] Finally, I had the privilege of editing and publishing Larry Walkemeyer's *A Good Walk Home*, an extended parable about the often painful tensions of living and dying well.

THE JAGGED JOURNEY: SOME BASICS

The unusual Walkemeyer work is about the art of dying. It acknowledges the classic work of Elizabeth Kübler-Ross on the stages of the standard journey people travel through the grief process.[7] This seasoned pastor then turns to the sayings of Jesus on the cross to get a little road map for the treacherous trip taken by the Master and later by his disciples. What constitutes a healthy, holy journey home? We're all on this trek whether we think much about it or not. What Jesus said and did shows us how to die and, maybe more importantly, how to live on the way to our eventual home.

Observes Walkemeyer at one point, "When one is wisely and well-prepared for death, then all the best of life lies ahead."[8] C. S. Lewis once added: "God whispers to us in our pleasures . . . and shouts in our pain."[9] So, careful attention to suffering may be the best way to the needed wisdom about dying and living.

Walking toward God's fullness of life is the best way to survive the jolts along the jagged faith journey. And jolts there will be. In Walkemeyer's book we encounter a "satisfaction spring" and a "reunion river," but also a "shadow valley," "confusion cave," and "reconciliation rocks." A smooth road is not promised for the traveling of the disciples of Jesus. What is promised are signposts along the way that say "8" and "9" and "10" (see chapters two and three). Follow them and the way becomes a sure road enabling a successful faith journey. It leads finally to the open arms of the loving Shepherd.

Along the way, however, being afflicted and blessing the Lord can and will go together. "I will bless the LORD at all times; his praise shall continually be in my mouth. My soul makes its boast in the LORD; let the afflicted hear and be glad. O magnify the LORD with me, and let us exalt his name together!" (Ps 34:1–3) That's what this book is all about, helping the afflicted to hear *and be glad*, despite whatever negative circumstance and unanswered questions obstruct the way.

I walked into a coffee shop and saw on the shelf some shiny bags for sale. I had no idea what was in them. On the outside it said, "THINK JERKY." My mind went somewhere other than to the grass-fed beef jerky on sale as convenient snacks. I thought of the irregular routes our lives typically take, proceeding in a very jerky manner, pulled one way and then another.

A friend emailed me. He was twenty-five, married just one week, and had just been told that he has cancer and will be "enjoying" his honeymoon between chemotherapy treatments. That was an abrupt twist in the trail he didn't expect or want! That's often how it goes for us fragile humans. Honeymoon and chemotherapy shouldn't but can go together.

Downton Abbey was an award-winning TV series pitting hundreds of years of British aristocracy against the tides of social upheaval and technical progress. It's set on the fictional Yorkshire country estate of Downton Abbey between 1912 and 1925. Depicted are the lives of the aristocratic Crawley family and their domestic servants. They strive to maintain a way of life that was slowly disintegrating. Who wants to watch a culture falling apart? Many people apparently.

By 2015 this series had become one of the more widely watched television drama shows in the world. Millions watched in many countries for six seasons. Why? Excellent writing, period costuming, and superb acting, yes, but there was more, including dramatic scenes of suffering, betrayal, war, pretension, passion, perversion, fire, frustration, etc. Convention was crumbling, a way of life shifting. It's an experience feared and understood in any culture at any time. Suffering is a constant experience, faith in God or not.

Should You Read On?

One would hope that the lives of Christians would be free of such destabilizing things as suffering in its many forms, but they are not. We can learn much from the long and troubled history of the Jews, the dramas of the early Christian church, and the many scared saints of the centuries. Chapter two dips into the mixed messages and truth anchors found in the Bible about suffering. Then chapter three highlights key wisdom to guide our travels on the jagged pathway of faith. Since the questions are not new, the best answers need not be created from scratch.

In fact, some aspects of our current times complicate good thinking about the difficult issues raised by suffering. The church, especially in the Western world, has become infused with constant thoughts of comfort, wellness, and peace with the surrounding society. There has been so much said by television preachers about a "prosperity gospel"—if I'm faithful to Jesus he will be faithful to me by giving me my fair share of health and wealth. Surely, it's wrongly argued, the Master doesn't want to be represented in an advanced culture by second-class citizens deeply disliked by the general public.

If that kind of thinking is yours, and you're satisfied with such "worldly" wisdom parading as the Christian gospel, please don't read on. You won't like what you find. You'll encounter unwelcome straight talk about suffering being central to God's own experience with the fallen creation and Christians very calling to be God's representatives. Assumed everywhere in what follows are two central truths which I understand to be at the heart of biblical revelation: (1) Suffering lies at the core of God's very being because of the divine love; and (2) Suffering is central to who Christians are supposed to be in this fallen world because of their imitating the ways of Jesus.

These central truths are hardly welcome in rich and self-seeking cultures, sometimes not even in the church that supposedly represents the loving God who self-sacrificed in Jesus Christ. They just don't fit and will never be popular, but there will be no compromise here. Truth is what it is, and we are supposed to be the disciples we are supposed to be, pain and all.

If you prefer to move through life with ease and expect God to lavish you with all good things as rewards for believing, find a different book to read—but beware. At some point, things will be very different than you think and want!

Living in Tension

If you will settle for only "clean" answers to complex questions, an approach to God and suffering free of mental tension, you won't find those here—or in the Bible. The two constant poles of the existing tension are these. (1) Suffering is very real, basic to the fallen human condition, including to followers of Jesus. (2) Suffering is not the last word; the last word is God's word of hope that there is the possibility of a suffering-free destiny beyond this fallen life. Christian faith stands between these poles, affirming both and seeking to serve present needs while living in the tension on the way.

Death and life form a constant continuum, the flower fading after it has bloomed beautifully. Bodies and whole societies bleed in great pain and cling to hope that soon the kingdom of God will be all in all. For Christian faith, the reality of the first must not be glossed over; and the hope of the second must somehow color all that we think and do.

What, then, is the difficult task of the faithful in the meantime, in the present time when suffering still goes on and the kingdom of rest and peace is still only an anticipation? It's "to be entirely realistic about the actuality of human suffering and at the same time affirm that the end of existence nevertheless transcends suffering."[10]

I have one final confession. This book was written in the United States, a place of relative comfort and safety, the place where some 5 percent of the world's people consume about 40 percent of the world's natural resources. In the West, the "developed" world, there is an extraordinary effort to keep the wretched out of public view. I've seen some of the worst in Africa with an AIDS orphan ministry I've served. Still, on an everyday basis, I've experienced and even seen little real suffering from which I wasn't safely insulated.

It's so easy for me, maybe the average North American, to break the tension, subtly denying suffering and focusing on the hope of heaven. However, to do so is to walk away from the compassionate God who is committed to the orphan and widow, to the starving and abused, to the spiritually empty and lost, to the suffering world that Christians are called to address in the name of Jesus. Our faith walk with the Master can be sure and heaven-bound, but being faithful to the high calling of God's ministering children will be a "jagged journey."

> If you will settle for only "clean" answers to complex questions, know that you won't find them here.

C. S. Lewis wrote *The Problem of Pain*, a superb treatment of suffering in the Christian life. Years later, after his wife had died of bone cancer, he wrote *A Grief Observed* under a pseudonym. A shattering experience had sobered and colored his perspective. He said, "You never know how much you really believe anything until its truth or falsehood becomes a matter of life and death to you."

Suffering comes. It's the jaggedness of the faith journey for individuals and the whole body of Christ. Any denying that the church will, even needs to suffer for the gospel of Christ will only add to the indifference of today's non-church public and the mass exodus of the young from the traditional church. Major research has revealed a few ideas on how to retain this departing generation.

One key idea is for Christian leaders to take risks, to really be the suffering church of Christ. As researcher David Kinnaman insists: "The radical shape of God's love is found at Christianity's pulsating core: the life, death, and resurrection of Jesus Christ. . . . Radical faith is about embodying the self-giving love of Jesus Christ—a love that risks suffering and matters more than life itself. Is Christianity worth the risk? Young people are watching and waiting to find out."[11]

I've lived a relatively conventional and "safe" faith life. Even so, I confess that I agree fully with Kinnaman. Suffering defines God's loving and risking heart on our behalf, and it defines our calling to be God's self-giving people in this present world. We see the people of God struggling throughout the Bible to come to terms with how suffering relates to God and the mission of God's people. The questions raised are many and, to be frank, the Bible appears to give mixed answers to some of them. It also gives a few truth anchors. To these we now turn.

2

BIBLICAL SIGNPOSTS

The Bible Gives Us Both Mixed Messages and Sure Anchors

God is completely sovereign, infinite in wisdom, and perfect in love. There is a dilemma related to this biblical teaching, however. It has been put this way: "God in his love always wills what is best for us. In his wisdom he always knows what is best, and in his sovereignty he has the power to bring it about."[12] But will God bring the best about, at least in the short-term? Apparently not.

We can say that all sin brings suffering, but we cannot turn the words inside out and say that all suffering comes from sin, even though this latter judgment dies a hard death.[13] Both viewpoints appear in the Bible among its mixed messages. Fortunately, the Bible also presents several sure anchors of truth.

The journey of God's people in this world has never been easy. After the tragic episode in the garden of Eden, pain, doubt, and toil have marked human life. Even so, the Bible insists that there is a path of faith that we can walk successfully and joyfully. It rises above the fear of delusion and doesn't collapse under the weight of despair, although it doesn't escape suffering. The path of the Christian sufferer is jagged as it tracks along the jolting terrain of life in this world.

This unfortunate circumstance of suffering is not optional. Even so, with God's guidance and resources available, it's a path that can be traveled successfully, yes, even joyfully. The journey is helped by a series of biblical signposts that keep us on track. Beware, however, that the road is not always clear. The messages sometimes appear mixed within the Bible itself. We do, however, find in the sacred pages a few anchors of truth that can stabilize our faith when the storms of life come.

The Biblical Pathway

Suffering is a subject that preoccupies many of the biblical writers. It comes up constantly in the Old Testament. In the New Testament, there may be more about suffering in church life than anything else. The books of 2 Corinthians, 1 Peter, and Revelation are dominated by the subject. The cross of Jesus, the high point of suffering and divine revelation, looks all the way back to the fall in Genesis and forward to the day when finally there will be no more tears.

We who believe in Jesus must resist the temptation to deny the jaggedness of the journey. American advertising bombards us with drugs, creams, injections, and cosmetic surgeries to alleviate our discomforts, improve our looks, and delay and finally mask death itself. We must resist embracing faith in ways that promise exemption from suffering—God supposedly guaranteeing health and prosperity to faithful people.

The true way of Jesus is *through* and not *around* suffering. Following and representing the man of sorrows in this troubled world can't happen by being successful and comfortable in worldly terms. We must not desire acceptance and applause and seek to avoid conflict with the principalities and powers opposing God's will and ways. That would be the irony of disciples directly denying their Master. So what is the biblical way of living faithfully?

One expression of this pot-holed but still possible pathway of suffering faith is found in 2 Corinthians 12:8–10. It forms the structure of this book (see the Table of Contents). It's the *8-9-10* path that travels from stability to despairing to rejoicing. It follows the pattern of the treacherous trail from gentle green grass to the valley of death and on to the home fold where the Shepherd cares for all things (Ps 23).

This *8-9-10* path is embedded in the whole book of Psalms. It jerks back and forth while always heading in the desired upward direction. One celebrated Bible scholar has called it the *O-D-R* path of faith, organizing the many psalms into three groups, Orientation, Disorientation, and Reorientation.[14]

The O-D-R path of the Psalms goes like this. First, things are as they should be, orientation. Then things go wrong, disorientation. But even when confusion and suffering are at their most intense, there arrives the grace and guidance of God to set our bleeding feet on higher ground than we had known before. We grow through the experience of being disoriented. We are graciously reoriented. Again, the path of the faith journey leads from comfortable stability to near despairing and on to fresh rejoicing.[15]

O-D-R is another way of looking at Paul's experience seen in 2 Corinthians 12:8–10. Our response to the suffering that comes along the jagged path of faith first tends (1) to either deny the pain or at least hope that somehow it will go away soon. Then it goes on (2) to a realization of the sufficiency of God in all circumstances, even the worst ones. Finally, it leads (3) to the amazing truth that even in our human weakness we can be increasingly strong. In fact, the weakness itself can become an instrument of growth and ministry.

It's along this jagged path that we learn the difficult reality of suffering and the amazing grace of God at work in its midst. Sometimes the faith walk can be a painful pilgrimage from life at risk to eternal life that transcends its many enemies by a healing power from beyond. The journey has its jaggedness and its joys.

> We don't find in the Bible a flurry of divine executive orders guaranteeing that God's will is always done precisely as planned.

Joining the psalmists, the Apostle Paul is our faithful guide. His testimony of the 8-9-10 trajectory was once offered to the Corinthians as a dependable map of finding the way to spiritual victory in a world of pain. It was Paul's personal history of ministry and misery and miracle. He had been given insight into "extravagant revelations" (2 Cor 12:7) while being subjected to numerous and painful set backs.

After Paul's great illumination on the road to Damascus came the beatings, escapes, floggings, shipwrecks, betrayals, and anxieties involved in assisting immature and even wayward churches. There were many long and sleepless nights. But somehow all of it became secondary to the dramatically positive side of Paul's overall growing experience. He'd been seized by Christ in a spiritual ecstasy, "hijacked into paradise." There, he reports, he had heard the unspeakable actually spoken.

Paul reports that he dared not brag about such amazing things. Actually, there was little danger of his "walking around high and mighty." He determines to say nothing more about himself than reporting his humiliations and a particular handicap. What that problem was we aren't told, and it doesn't matter. It was an ongoing suffering given "to keep me in constant touch with my limitations" (2 Cor 12:7). This grateful apostle traveled on through all the jaggedness with increasing gratitude and joy.

Suffering certainly will keep one humble. At first Paul begged God to remove the problem, likely malaria or epilepsy. He'd heard back only that God's grace is sufficient and the strength of God eventually would shine through his weakness and always be adequate for his need. Once he accepted this, Paul actually began to almost appreciate his problem. "It was a case of Christ's strength moving in on my weakness. Now I take limitations in stride, and with good cheer, these limitations that cut me down to size" (2 Cor 12:9).

Paul's *8-9-10* path went from resistance and maybe even denial to the heights of faith, then to near despair and finally, strangely, surprisingly, to ultimate rejoicing. To use the *O-D-R* imagery, there are seasons of orienting satisfaction, periods of disorienting suffering, and resurrection surprises. The trip is anything but pure vacation, but it's survivable and even a source of unexpected joy and fresh life. Eventually, amazingly, wonderfully, the path leads to spiritual maturity and to our eternal home. It's much like tracking the life, death, and resurrection of Jesus. We learn from his life and teachings, we are shocked by his brutal death, and then we rejoice in the wonderful news of his resurrection. We get oriented, disoriented, and reoriented.

Our days with the Lord alternate among (1) being settled in and stabilized by faith, (2) being shocked, confused, and disoriented by negative events, and finally (3) being newly assured of the adequacy of God's goodness and grace in any circumstance, even the worst. Is there an easier way? No. Can money or connections avoid pain by purchasing pleasures? Maybe, momentarily. Can the journey of faith, jagged as it is, be completed successfully? Yes!

There's plenty of biblical help available. The psalms of the ancient Jews probe every possible pitfall and point to the best way through to our final home. They "correspond to seasons of human life and bring those seasons to speech.... They affirm that if we try to keep our lives we will lose them, and that when lost for the gospel, we will be given life (Mark 8:35)."[16]

The Jews, although God's own people, surely knew well the jagged journey. They were enslaved in Egypt, exiled in Babylon, and embattled and occupied by one alien empire after another. And then the Jew of all Jews, Jesus the gentle Lamb of God, was brutally executed by the Romans although guilty of nothing except bringing loving good news to this world.

On the subject of suffering, then, Jesus and his fellow Jews may be our greatest teachers of all. We have to read carefully their stories, however. The Bible can be seen as sending mixed messages about the source and meaning of suffering and the action or inaction of God in relation to it.

Mixed Messages

I wrote these lines during a two-week journey from Rome to Florida by sea. My wife and I were cruising on the beautiful Royal Princess with a consistent message directed our way—luxury. Another message was never far away. The captain would come on the communication system at noon each day and remind us of the depth of the water below our hull—sometimes approaching 20,000 feet! Twice in the Atlantic Ocean we had to be careful to skirt hurricanes. The ocean floor far beneath is riddled with vessels and lives lost from the ravages of past weather, accidents, and wars.

If only life and even the Bible didn't give us mixed messages! Death and life, perishing and cruising, poverty and luxury, pain and joy, heights of insight and depths of danger. Paul said, "Though our outward man perish, yet the inward man is renewed day by day" (2 Cor 4:16). But here's where the mixed messages start forcing their way in. What if the perishing is happening and the renewing isn't? What if the psalmist's fear is coming true, "Take not Thy Holy Spirit from me" (Ps 51:11)?

To have the Spirit is to have God's eyes within, helping us see beyond the darkness to the dawn that God's grace might yet make possible. Notice the word *might*. What if there is no Spirit apparently present? To lose the Spirit is to grow skeptical about faith, empty without hope, spiritually blind, desperate because pain and loss are smothering life itself, leaving an aching blank where the pulsating Spirit once was. The Bible records much despair and also shines with much more hope. Is suffering the occasion for the ending or the deepening of faith? It's our choice.

We act variously and the Bible speaks variously. The book of Proverbs tends to emphasize the justice of suffering and how suffering often is directly related to wrongdoing. On the other hand, Job and Ecclesiastes insist that much suffering is unjust and irrational. Proverbs maintains that righteousness is rewarded and sin punished (e.g., Prov 1:29–33). But Job's experience is a frontal assault on such a simplistic assessment of things.

Since the Bible, when taken as a whole, presents the full picture of things, we must be careful not to isolate one biblical passage or even verse from many others on the same subject. For instance, Jeremiah 29:10 by itself leads to believing that God has planned in advance and detail all things that happen in this world. Reading Ezekiel 34 and many passages like it, however, would convince us that God's interventions in this world are not pre-planned but responses to negative circumstances we have created.

Life in this world is hardly a lovely fairy tale of predictable patterns of experience. Sometimes the just suffer and the unjust prosper. Sometimes God intervenes and sometimes God remains silent and inactive so far as we can tell. So, why not take the advice of Job's wife—curse God and die? Because the jagged path of faith, even while meandering through valleys of dark shadows, occasionally bursts with sunlight, suggesting a way out, a way upward to the shining heights of eternal joy.

Progress on this path of faith doesn't come quickly or easily. Patience, discipline, selfless service, and enduring the jagged journey are required. The goal is earned, not given cheaply. Four unwelcome things are interwoven into the very pattern of our human existence. Closing our eyes to them changes nothing except our ability to face them well. They are suffering, evil, injustice, and a keen awareness of how brief are our years.

Two great pieces of music are sharply contrasting and so revealing when experienced together. They represent two basic options for viewing God, suffering, and the life of faith. Tchaikovsky's great *B Minor Symphony* is full of marching rhythms that move inexorably toward the end of tragic desolation. The composer described this music's theme as "the haunting of life by death." On the other hand, Brahms' great *Requiem*, while still having death as a theme, lacks the pessimism. Its somber mood eventually merges into the great climaxes of peace and victory.

Fatalism is always an option, a sad giving in to the awful abyss. Faith also is an option, a daring reach upward that allows the poor pilgrim to find God as guide, resource, and eternal home. These pages choose Brahms, faith, and the reach upward. This doesn't make suffering and death evaporate, not in this world at least. But it does what we really need. It allows us to survive, even thrive in the midst of whatever. When things are falling apart, we can believe even before seeing positive results. God already is putting the broken pieces together into some new and yet unfinished masterpiece.

God's Sovereignty and Reasons for Suffering

There's a big theological divide not easy to navigate. Christians across the centuries have stood on both sides. The Bible doesn't help us as much as it might. Again, it seems to give mixed messages, or at least allows two contrasting streams of its own interpretation by equally honest and careful readers. It comes down to a definition of God's sovereignty.

Divine "sovereignty" is a central subject of Christian believing, with two contrasting streams of biblical interpretation. The complicating fact is that, conscious of it or not, we tend to bring to our Bible reading preconceived notions that color what we read and how we understand. We bring our theology to the biblical text and read through our preset theological eyes.

I experienced strong exposure to both streams of interpretation early in life. I studied Bible at Geneva College, a fine institution rooted in the Scottish Presbyterian tradition strongly influenced by the theologian John Calvin. Then I attended Anderson University School of Theology and Asbury Theological Seminary, graduate schools rooted more in the English tradition strongly influenced by John Wesley. These two outstanding Protestant thinkers and reformers had much in common theologically, with at least one significant exception. It centers in Wesley's resistance to Calvin's conclusion that God determined in advance that some persons would be saved and others not.

Both of these Protestant leaders agreed that "nothing in heaven or earth is understood properly except in light of the divine Parent who brought it into being, who is its ground and goal, who is sovereign, fully able, fully faithful, full of justice and mercy."[17] Calvin's logic concluded that God's sovereignty must mean that God is always in full control of all things, including our daily affairs and future destinies. Wesley found this an unacceptable outcome of biblical logic, a picturing of God as other than seen in the coming of Jesus, the one who said that God deeply desires that all be saved.

The core question is this. Does divine sovereignty, with unlimited capacities, imply that God retains and exercises full control of all earthly events? Are we "predestined"?

Wesley and Calvin agreed on two things, but not a third. They agreed that fallen humanity is incapable of doing anything to merit salvation, and thus all salvation is by God's grace alone. They disagreed, however, on one key point. Wesley insisted that God wants all to be saved and has provided the "prevenient" grace that enables all to choose salvation. Each person is enabled to respond and therefore responsible for the choice made. Any who do not choose salvation face damnation by their own choice and not by God's advance decree.[18]

The provision of such free choice, Wesley insisted, does not undercut divine sovereignty but *defines it*, dramatizing the preeminence of God's love (see below the section "Love Trumps Power"). Such a preeminence of love is critical for how people should understand the source of their sufferings and their opportunity for salvation in spite of them.

I have pictured this Calvin-Wesley divide as the clash of flowers. Calvin's *TULIP* includes the "L" of "limited atonement." Wesley's contrasting ROSE sees the biblically revealed God as **R**elational, **O**pen, **S**uffering, and **E**verywhere Active. His flower model is more relational, experiential, and loving in tone and manner, and it highlights the central role of suffering—ours, the world's, and even God's. Yes, even the sovereign God suffers.

I was privileged to author the biography of prominent Canadian theologian Clark H. Pinnock, who traveled the jagged journey of first championing Calvin's view of divine sovereignty and later being a prominent exponent of Wesley's view.[19] On this key subject, I am a Wesleyan along with Pinnock and many others. That influences my biblical understanding and these present pages.

God willingly, out of the love that is God's very nature, chooses to relate interactively and redemptively with this fallen creation. God is open to freely made human decisions and suffers along with the creation when the wrong decisions are made. God risks this awkward process by choice because the preeminent perfection of God's sovereignty is *love*. God, being sovereign, is capable of acting only in ways consistent with his own nature and intentions. God's nature is love and the loving intention is that all be saved.

We fallen people are struggling in this failing world. We are on jagged journeys. We are enabled by God's grace to choose for or against God, including choices that bring suffering to ourselves and others, and even our own damnation. God enables and allows, loves and suffers when poor choices are made.

BIBLICAL SIGNPOSTS

MODELS OF DIVINE PROVIDENCE

TULIP

Total Depravity

  Unconditional Election

    Limited Atonement

      Irresistable Grace

        Perserverance of the Saints

ROSE

Relational, not aloof

  Open, present, interactive

    Suffering, affected by our sin

      Everywhere Active, saving grace for all

Where did the fallenness come from? Is God still in control? If so, does being in control mean that God is in charge of and even responsible for all events, even the most evil ones? The Bible is clear about God's existence, but it's interpreters have been less agreed on what it teaches about *how* God chooses to relate to the world's fallenness. Several best-selling books highlight two contrasting options.

Love Trumps Power

Here's the first option for understanding how the Bible says God deals with the results of human fallenness, and thus who is responsible for our present suffering. Jerry Bridges keys his thinking off of Isaiah 38:17 where King Hezekiah decides, "surely it was for my benefit that I suffered such anguish." God's presence and sovereignty are said to be always present and active and in full control of all events in human history, even when they are turning sharply downward. Presumably, all that happens is for the eventual benefit of God's chosen people, even when events look quite otherwise. All was planned in advance. God has absolute independence and absolute control over the actions of all creatures.[20]

Bridges also points to Lamentations 3:37, "Who can speak and have it happen if the Lord has not decreed it?" and to Isaiah 45:7, "I form the light and create darkness, I bring prosperity and create disaster; I, the Lord, do all these things." This is a power position. God has all the power and uses it to accomplish the divine will in this world. All is pre-planned and fully controlled.

Here's the contrasting option, one I think more biblical when the whole of biblical revelation is considered. When ultimate *power* is set forth as the primary attribute of God, no answer will be satisfying to the persistent question, why does God not eliminate awful suffering when God can with his power and should with his goodness? The answer is that Bible puts divine power in the context of God's love relationship with his beloved.

God is said to be *love*. Love is God's *primary perfection*, not power. God's use of power is disciplined by God's loving nature. This implies that God tends to withhold acts of divine *coercion* in favor of the wooing of reaching and redeeming love. God is powerfully present in all events, to be sure, but without the choice of dictating and fully controlling them.

Insists Douglas John Hall in contrast to Jerry Bridges, "There is no sword that can cut away sin without killing the sinner. . . . Freedom is of the very essence of the human creature. . . . *Jesus* is the Christ."[21] The implication of this final claim is that God works against evil in this world in the way portrayed in the crucifixion of Jesus. Divine wisdom is that of the cross (1 Cor 1—2). Therefore, "the only power that can address suffering humanity is the power of love, and that is a power 'made perfect in weakness'" (2 Cor 12:9).

Many verses, especially in the Old Testament, can be quoted on the side of Bridges—strict divine control, which seems to imply that God is at fault when evil events are unstopped. But the Christian should follow the Master who said he did not come to destroy but to fulfill his Jewish tradition. In fulfilling it, he often corrected its common teaching traditions, especially by turning law into a *love focus*. Jesus ended the sacrificing and suffering of animals by placing God on the altar once and for all! The great love of God was willing to suffer. God *self-sacrificed* on our behalf! That's the very heart of Christian faith. True and undeserved love redeems our lives and sets us on the jagged journey of loving others.

Admittedly, it's hard to get away from the focus on divine power. Much Christian theology over the centuries has been formed while the church was existing as a prominent center of power in various worldly empires. It's been observed that a "prestigious" church, Christianity as the official religion of an empire, can hardly afford to be known as representative of a crucified God! Women theologians have rightly told us recently that for much too long the church has highlighted the power manner of God's working, reflecting an excessively male reading of the Bible and an unbalanced masculine way of being in the world.

Could it be that, in our day when the church is being reduced to much less prominence in secularized societies, she could rediscover her true self? If so, a power focus would give way to the more biblical *love focus*. The Bible would stop being read as God coercively marching in triumph over all enemies and conquering all suffering and evil by mighty power, even by pre-planning all events. It would be read as intended, God in Christ reaching in love to make possible the redemption of all the lost, Christ through his Spirit working through suffering in the midst of our suffering to bring good out of evil.

If we read the Bible through the eyes of God's love, not through a dominance of God's power and judgment, the TULIP theological metaphor of Calvin yields to the ROSE of Wesley. We then come to better understand why evil manages to happen even in God's world. We come to see more clearly that those who gain new life in Christ, through the graciousness of the Father's love, are called to join in the ministry of suffering and self-sacrificing love. When in pain ourselves or seeing a great injustice crippling others, we come to be less inclined to place blame on the victim ("you're getting what you deserve") or blame God for allowing it in the first place when the power was available to force justice.

We also should note the celebrated book *When Bad Things Happen to Good People*. Rabbi Kushner deals with suffering in his family and among the many to whom he had ministered over the years. He comes to some radical conclusions, or are they just so different from how people often think that we judge them radical? He certainly champions the love focus of God, which for him leads to some dramatic conclusions.

"Our being human [by God's design] leaves us free to hurt each other, and God can't stop us without taking away the freedom that makes us human." So, God couldn't stop Hitler from his monstrous evil. "God wants justice and fairness but can't always arrange for them." Is God the source of evil happenings? Absolutely not! "God is as outraged as we are." "The God I believe in does not send us the problem; He gives us the strength to cope with the problem." The God who "neither causes nor prevents tragedies helps by inspiring people to help."[22] It's the way love works.

Again, there are two options before us for reading the workings of God. I choose the ROSE-like one, God the compassionate lover over God the judgmental wielder of power. Why? Because in Christ we have received God's own self-revelation. God works in the way most consistent with the divine nature and intent, and both are seen hanging on the cross of Jesus.

But, even when this understanding is firmly in place, there may be exceptions, unanswered questions, and occasions when the power option prevails. Rabbi Kushner may be essentially right and yet somewhat wrong when insisting that God "can't" act forcefully against evil. In fact, the Bible records numerous examples of God doing just that. These examples are real if only the exceptions to God's preferred way of working.

Pivot Points and Truth Anchors

People commonly see what appears to be the Bible's mixed messages about the causes of suffering and the related action or inaction of God. Some people can't tolerate anything mixed coming from the Bible and choose one aspect of the whole to be the final and only biblical answer. This reaction is very human, and yet it also is very unfair to the Bible, which sees the whole picture, reports the whole, and in the midst of it all gives a few sure anchors to allow safe passage through the maze. Here are the orienting, dependable, and clearly biblical anchors of truth.

> The Bible sees the whole of life, reports the whole, and gives sure anchors to allow safe passage through the maze.

Anchor #1. Love, Not Coercion.

What about all the grotesque and dehumanizing suffering we see or at least hear of constantly? The answer isn't easy for believers in a God who is believed to be all good and all-powerful. It lies somewhere on the line connecting "intends" and "allows." The Sovereign of all is also the Lover of all who surely intends only good for all. Then why does any awful suffering ever exist?

We know this much from the Bible. God is a risking Lover who *allows* suffering by giving freedom of choice to us humans. This is a love gift that necessarily includes the possibility of its misuse, sin. God never *intends* sin or suffering. It comes from our choosing not to love in response to God's love. The divine intention is that humans freely choose a loving relationship with God and each other. Since that obviously has gone sour by human choice, God reacts in love while allowing the negative results of our wrong choices to play out.

The major reaction of God, however, is to choose in Christ to enter into the arena of our suffering in order to share the suffering and work to bring good out of the evil we have created. In this "incarnating" process, God never gives up sovereign control of the creation. Nothing in the creation can ultimately frustrate what God intends. In the meantime, however, we creatures have much to say about how our history goes. It often goes badly, bringing suffering even to the innocent, even to God. That's how the biblical story goes.

What God allows includes the awful cross of Jesus, with something about that cross needing to be made clear. It's a dramatic picture of the bleeding heart and reaching love of God the Father. "The Cross was no more the will of God than any other brutal murder. It was the work of wicked men."[23] Christians often have insisted that God planned the death of the Son all along, even that the death was necessary for the forgiveness of our sins—an extension of the tradition of animal sacrifice. On biblical grounds, I argue otherwise.

Our well-being and loving relationship with God have been God's plan all along. God's reaching love has infused that plan. Self-giving sacrifice has been at the heart of God's very identity from the eternities. Our sin forced its activation in Christ on our behalf. In that sense, the cross was "planned," but only in that sense. The cross was a heavy price for God to pay for our sins. It was the bleeding heart of the divine dripping healing and forgiveness on our broken souls.

Here's what is shown so dramatically on that cross of Jesus. *Love does not coerce.* The power of God is to be seen through the lens of God's love. God allows evil because God's nature is love. Love instructs, persuades, and disciplines, but coerces only as a last resort. One might say that evil cannot be forcibly stopped without violating the free choice of humans—which would make us marionettes and not potential love partners with God. This necessity of allowing our free choices is not to be seen as a "limitation" of God's power; it's merely an acknowledgment of who God really and always is.

Anchor #2. Divine Patience.

Note this brief dialogue I once created between God and the whale over how best to handle the wayward Jonah:

> **God:** "There's a guy with an assignment from me who hasn't the stomach for it. He's being sent to Nineveh and choosing selfishly to head in the wrong direction. I want your help."
>
> **Wally (the whale):** "I say, why don't you smack him in the face and make him pay attention without bothering me? You're the biggest thing in the whole creation, not me!"
>
> **God:** "Sorry, Wally, but I've decided you're just the ticket. I'm not the smacking type, at least not at first."[24]

What's the point? God has smacking capacity and is known to use it in extreme circumstances—tough love. Some suffering may come from being forcibly punished by God for sinning. However, God typically chooses to begin with the softer love option, patience over sheer power. God's heart is love and love's first option for dealing with our sin is persuasion not coercion. It's usually patience before power.

Philip Yancey puts his finger right on this biblical anchor of truth. The Bible is full of examples of much divine patience going before direct and coercive punishment. "The people of Israel knew why they were being punished; the prophets had warned them in excruciating detail. The Pharaoh of Egypt knew exactly why the ten plagues were unleashed against his land: God had predicted them, told him why, and described what change of heart could forestall them. Biblical examples of suffering-as-punishment, then, tend to fit a pattern. The pain comes after much warning, and no one sits around afterward asking, 'Why?' They know very well why they are suffering."[25]

Anchor #3. Looking Forward.

We must get beyond any preoccupation with demanding answers to the "why" questions of suffering. We suffering humans typically ask the wrong questions. We want to know why something bad has happened. Where did it come from? Who's responsible? Am I guilty of something? The Bible, however, consistently moves to another question, the forward-looking "What now?" in favor of the backward-looking "Who caused this?" and "Why me?"

Suffering, whatever its unclear cause in a given instance, has the capacity of producing something of value if that's where our focus goes. Pain can be newly woven into something freshly beautiful. What is bad can be channeled into something good never possible before. Since that's precisely what the loving and redeeming God is always about, surely that's where our attention should be.

We'll consider in later chapters how suffering can be managed constructively and even used for our training in Christ-likeness—a major goal of all biblical revelation. In the meantime, we should avoid the "why" in favor of the "what." I may not know *why* this or that is happening, but with God's help I can learn *what* good might come out of it if my focus is in that direction.

Anchor #4. Hope Persists Regardless.

Shaking loose of the disabling "why" questions and looking forward expectantly is possible because God is at work in this world whatever the circumstances. The point of the empty tomb of Jesus is that the worst that can happen in this life never has to be the end of the story. We are emboldened to believe that new possibilities exist because of the grace of God. Even death can die!

The call of Christ is for the faithful to fix their gaze on the positive potential lodged in the negative. Suffering has been overwhelmed by victory, and even can be used as a tool that helps bring victory. Jesus has died and also risen. New can emerge from old.

This is illustrated repeatedly in the Bible. The final editors of the present Bible appear to have had a structural agenda designed for our encouragement. The major units of the biblical material all tend to end *on the same note*. The worst has happened, *but* . . . . Here's a quick run through the whole Bible, pointing out this repeating note at the end of each major unit of material.

1. **Torah.** Moses dies, but Joshua lives! God's people will enter their promised land even though Moses will not (Deut 34:4).
2. **Prophets.** For those who finally honor God, sunrise is coming. The arrogant will be burned up and God's people will burst with energy and dance with joy! (Mal 4:1–3).
3. **Writings.** The Exile has been long and awful, but suddenly the new king Cyrus says, "Now it's time to go home and rebuild. It's over. You are free!" (2 Chr 36:22–23).
4. **Gospels.** Do you want to be part of God's coming future? Be good stewards of today. Feed my sheep! (John 21:17–19). Meanwhile, I go to prepare an eternal place for you. Knowing that, you can go on with your work here.
5. **Letters.** How can we be sure that we can manage in evil times and that the future is secure? Because the God who promises is full of glory, majesty, strength, and rule before all time, and now, and to the end of all time. Yes! (Jude 1:24–25).
6. **End of All Ends.** When will relief be real for us who still wait and suffer? Says Jesus, the Alpha and Omega, "I'm on my way! I'll be there soon! Yes! Come, Master Jesus! The grace of the Master Jesus be with all of you. Oh, Yes!" (Rev. 22:20–21).

It's a constant note in the Bible. Hope persists regardless of circumstance because the loving God persists, prevails, and promises.

Anchor #5. Head Toward the World's Suffering.

God is love in eternal being and thus in earthly action. The people of God are to join the divine action by being filled with God's Spirit and focusing their attention where God's attention is focused. We are to love as God loves.

Whatever the philosophical debates about the origins of suffering, God's focus is on doing something about it in the present that we are experiencing. Suffering is central to the fact and meaning of God-with-us in Jesus. It's also central to the intended reality of our lives of faith. We are to represent Jesus in this evil-laden and suffering world by relieving the suffering of others, even at the cost of our own suffering.

Some pain is intended by the Creator. There is, after all, a pain that makes *becoming* possible—see chapters ten and eleven. But much of the suffering that now exists surely was not intended by a loving God because it works only toward destruction. It's just "evil," "live" spelled backwards. Again, we must put an end to the "why" questions and shift to doing God's healing work. What did Jesus tell his disciples on that Mount of Transfiguration? I'll paraphrase. "You can't stay here forever absorbing this spiritual high, protected from the pain. Go back down to the masses who suffer. Get your hands dirty and feed my sheep!"

The Heart of Biblical Revelation

The resurrection of Jesus made plain that God had been *with* us and *for* us as the Son hung and died on the cross. The empty tomb means that the cross is never the end of the story of Jesus or of ourselves and our suffering. We certainly haven't been given all the explanations about the causes of suffering in particular cases. Mystery remains. What we do know is that darkness already has been overwhelmed by light. Given the resurrection, even the cross glows with glory! That doesn't answer all of our questions, admittedly, but it does point in the right direction and brings hope to the jaggedness of our faith journey.

This is the heart of biblical revelation and thus of Christian faith. What's God's primary response to human suffering? It's God's *personal identification with it in Christ*. The main answer to the problem of pain is the *pain of God*. We must not shy from the thought of God in pain. You'll find this quote elsewhere in the book: "God's problem is not that God is not *able* to do certain things. God's problem is that God *loves*! Love complicates the life of God as it complicates every life."

This loving complication means that God's *power* ultimately reveals itself "in divine solidarity with the sufferer, that is, in the 'weakness' of suffering love."[26] God really was *with us* in the suffering of Jesus. God wasn't only remotely with us in Jesus' suffering and death, there by proxy and at a safe distance, only illustratively. God really and fully was there as *Emmanuel*, "God with us." We typically speak of the sacrifice of Jesus when actually we should dare to say more. God in Jesus was *self-sacrificing* as an act of amazing love.

The cosmic significance of the cross is this. God the Father was choosing to meet our suffering with that of his own, addressing the suffering caused by our sin with presence and personal pain. Because of the depth of divine love, God was voluntarily participating in our suffering, the innocent suffering for the guilty, in order that the pain of our guilt could be purged of divine judgment and cleansed of final power over our existence and destiny. The big words are *incarnation*, voluntarily assuming and suffering in our flesh, and *atonement*, suffering in our flesh so that we again could be *at one* with God.

> The Cross of Jesus, high point of suffering and divine revelation, looks back to the fall in Genesis and forward to the day when there will be no more tears.

To see this God on the cross is to know this God's true heart. The cross should cause us to love this God, turning from sin and receiving forgiveness and new life. But it's always our choice. We can look at amazing love and melt in full repentance. We also can look, hate on, and die an unnecessary death. If we receive and are renewed by divine love, what happens to us? Seeing the suffering love that is God, we are enabled to become agents of that love in a suffering world. We are to become models here and now of what God is always and everywhere. We will never be God, of course, but with God in us and serving through us we can function as apostles of divine love.

Given where Christ now is, at God's right hand, where are we to be if filled with Christ's Spirit? We are being drawn *toward the suffering of the world*, just as God was and is. Suffering love is a reality at God's very heart and also at the center of our calling as God's children. Karl Rahner once put it well in an Easter homily:

> Christ is already in the midst of all the poor things of this earth, which we cannot leave because it is our mother.... He is in all

tears and in all death as hidden rejoicing and as the life which triumphs by appearing to die. He is in the beggar to whom we give, as the secret wealth which accrues to the donor. He is in the pitiful defeats of his servants as the victory which is God's alone. He is in our powerlessness as the power which can allow itself to seem weak because it is unconquerable.[27]

Beautifully said! Given the loving heart of God now shared at great cost for us, where and how should we be as God's faithful children? We are to be with those who are suffering just as God has graciously been with us.

Biblical faith reports that who God is and what God has done and is doing is for the sake of this creation. The new creation in the blood of Christ is intended only secondarily to "get people to heaven." Primarily, it's intended to make the disciples of Jesus "responsible, grateful, and joyful citizens of earth."[28] God being with and identifying with us brings pain to God; our identifying lovingly in God's name with this creation and its troubles will bring pain to us. *So be it!* So says the entire Bible with its signposts and truth anchors.

3

THE PATH AHEAD

God Will Show the Way Even When There Appears to Be No Way

We learn something important as we move along the jagged pathway of Christian faith. Resurrection trumps crucifixion!

One reason why it's so hard to understand the will of God is that there are three of them.

The Christian community relies on the Bible for its primary understanding of the revelation of God. We saw in the previous chapter that this sacred source speaks often about suffering. There are some mixed messages. There also are several sure truth anchors for our thinking and believing. Relying on these anchors, we now will identify key elements of belief that helpfully orient us as we travel the jagged path of faith throughout our lives in this troubled world. Together they form the basics of a Christian theology of suffering and authentic discipleship.

The Threefold Path

Suffering penetrates and shapes the very meaning and trajectory of Christian faith. In our personal experiences it tends to follow the threefold *8-9-10* path of 2 Corinthians 12:8-9-10. The experienced trajectory of a Christian's suffering moves through the troubled terrain of a life of faith in this broken world. It goes from verse 8 (we say: "Take the Pain Away!"), to verse 9 (God says: "My Grace is Sufficient!"), and finally leads to verse 10 (the fact is: "Weakness Can Be Strength!"). We who belong to Christ can go from shock and denial (v. 8), to a greater awareness of the divine dimensions of the situation (v. 9), and finally to our being transformed into the image of Jesus, allowing God's love to be realized in and ministered through us in spite of and sometimes even with the help of suffering (v. 10).

St. Paul pioneered this trail of tears and triumphs. He once was addressing the church in Corinth that needed his witness in the midst of its severe troubles. The witness came in the form of his own reported life paradox, the pit of human experience (thorn in the flesh) and its pinnacle (being transported into the highest heaven). He begged God to have the first removed, but it wasn't. He was careful not to boast inappropriately about the latter, even though God was lavishing goodness on him in the midst of his suffering. A resurrection had overwhelmed Paul's cross with a glow of glory. He had learned that there can be gain in loss, and that all gain is by God's pure grace.

> Wherever the snake came from that seduced Adam and Eve, and whatever mischief it's still creating, know that its head is already cut off!

Christians have chosen the cross of Jesus as a central symbol. Why? Because it represents the dramatic redemptive act of God and the full range of the experience of those faithful to Jesus. We humans are fragile beings. When following Jesus, we find ourselves out of step with the world as it now is. Our weakness is real and we are not promised a free pass through trouble. On the other hand, the crucified Jesus is no longer hanging in death, nor should we be terrified of a cross for ourselves.

The story of Jesus did not end when his tortured breathing ceased. *Resurrection trumps crucifixion.* Here is theological wisdom. "To the New Testament, pain is not morbidity or hopelessness or retribution. It is still the devil's work, but the devil has been overcome and the penalty has been cancelled. So pain is now cleansing, illumination, and vocation. . . . The Event of Christ has changed the bitter waters into a pool of healing."[29]

The later chapters of this book attempt to explain how the bitterness can be transformed into healing and how suffering should become our calling as Christians. To be a true Christian is to walk a special and often rocky path. Suffering will be part of it. Some have called the suffering "apostolic,"

IMAGES OF THE JAGGED JOURNEY

8-9-10   2 Corinthians 12:8-10

When trouble comes...

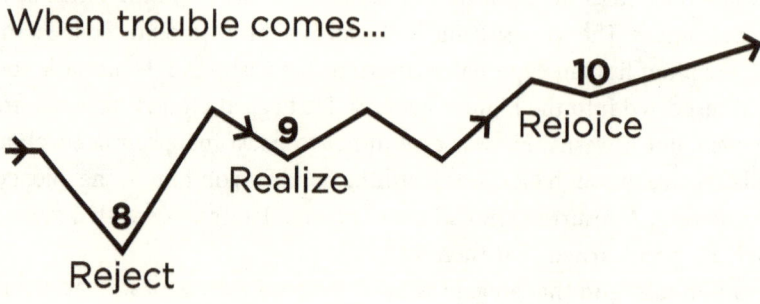

O-D-R   Book of Psalms

When life goes wrong...

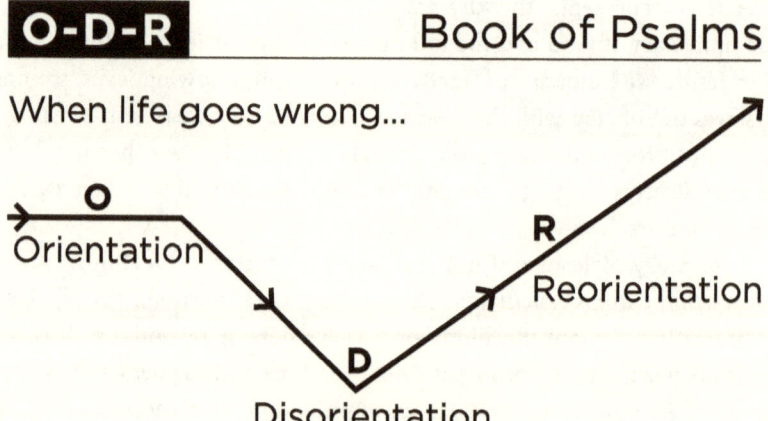

that is, we will be speaking and acting and being treated *like Jesus*. Again, so be it!

The Christian's jagged faith and discipleship journey is paralleled on the larger scene by God's own journey. What is the will of God for events on our earthly scene? The answer is not simple to state. There is the *threefold will of God* (see below). Not being clear about this is responsible for a rash of unnecessary and troubling questions people ask constantly, especially when suffering.

Did God cause the disaster or bring my suffering to me? Why didn't God stop it from happening in the first place? Does God control everything in this world? If all-powerful, how could God not be in full control? What is the usual way of God's working in our tragic situations? Is it through divine love or divine power? See the ROSE metaphor in chapter two and the explanation below of the threefold divine will. They are both critical to addressing these questions and walking successfully the *8-9-10* path of suffering.

Dimensions of the Divine Will

Classic ("orthodox") Christianity speaks often and clearly about our present suffering and God's present working. Obviously there is some variety in this speaking, like the mixed messages we find in the Bible. But also, again like the Bible, there are some key anchors of belief that have received broad consensus. Here is a brief summary of this consensus as reported in the masterful work *Classic Christianity,* by Thomas Oden.

1. "God's will is the effective energy inherent in God by which God is able to do all things consistent with the divine nature."[30] There are no "limits" on the actions of God other than the divine nature itself, which is *love*. God is Person and has created persons to share in loving relationship with God. This ultimate will of God never changes regardless of what we humans do.

2. An essential element of personhood is freedom to choose and act accordingly. Humans have been granted such freedom by the loving God. The wrong use of freedom is the source of much of the evil in this now-fallen world. Despite the current circumstances of our human history and personal lives, God remains free to express the divine loving will, but necessarily now within the changing conditions of our

freely chosen history (Ps 40:8; Matt 6:10; John 7:17). See below for an explanation of the threefold will of God.

3. When we humans act counter to God's loving intentions for us, God remains fully able and committed to taking our idolatries and sins and making them work toward the greater good God intends, all to God's glory and our good. Such contingent divine actions may be viewed as the "consequent" will of God, God's strategic adjustments appropriate to the historical challenges, failures, and sufferings that we cause by misuse of our freedom (Heb 10: 5–10). Human willing is able to resist the will of God, but temporarily, never ultimately.

We will use these perspectives as essential theological markers to understand our walking on the jagged pathway of faith. They arise naturally from the anchoring truth perspectives found in the Bible and our resulting inclination to favor the ROSE over the TULIP model of understanding God's sovereignty (see chapter two). They also are fully consistent with the *threefold* understanding of God's will.

It was in the terrible war year of 1944 that Leslie D. Weatherhead shared unusual wisdom with his City Temple congregation in ravaged England. Suffering was everywhere and so were the questions about how God was related to a reeling world at war. What was God's will for the suffering English people, not to mention the terrible plight of the Jews on the continent? Surely God did not intend the awful evil seen everywhere. But if the mass suffering was not God's will, how did it manage to happen? Was God really in control or was the will of God being defeated by the forces of evil?

The answer from Weatherhead came in the form of his explanation of the threefold will of God. This understanding can be of great comfort to the sufferer tempted to blame herself or God when neither is actually at fault. Published in the book *The Will of God*,[31] Weatherhead describes the three dimensions of the divine will as follows.

1. **God's Intentional Will.** Consistent desires and actions always flow from the loving heart of God toward us humans. They are God's deliberate intentions for us, the ideal plan, the goal of creation, that which is intentional on God's part. They center in the intention that none be lost from God's loving care, and that we all be in right relationship with God and each other now and eternally (Matt 18:14).

However, human sin has intervened in the creation by our free choice as haughty humans. So it's now the case that much that happens to God's beloved was never intended. It's crucial that we who suffer realize that more is operating in this world than God's loving will. Sin has brought ruin in its wake. Therefore, God adapts the loving divine strategy for accomplishing divine intentions, working in new circumstances, evil circumstances of our own making. Divine intentions have not changed; human circumstances have.

2. **God's Circumstantial Will.** The love of God requires that freedom be given to us humans and not be violated by the overriding of coercive divine actions. In the current circumstances of this fallen world, with all of our bad choices and their bad results for us and others, God reluctantly accepts and allows and adapts. Since God's intentional will remains in place, love keeps working toward it regardless of circumstances pulling the other way. God does not limit the free will given to us, reducing us to a sub-human status, but maintains our dignity in the midst of our costly choosing. Consequently, many will suffer and some will be lost forever despite God's great redeeming love (1 Cor 1:18).

The "omnipotence" of God does not mean that, by sheer exhibitions of superior might, God always gets his own way. If God did, human freedom would be an illusion and our moral development would be impossible. No "end" that God has in mind can be imposed forcibly from without. God's intended goal, the reconciliation or at-one-ment (atonement) of all souls, must come from our choice of God's way, not the imposition of God's will by irresistible force.

Power means the ability to achieve purpose. Since the purpose of God is to gain our grateful acceptance of the divine love, any coercive activity of God's which denies or suppresses our free choice would defeat the purpose. It would not be a successful use of divine power but a confession of divine weakness and an acceptance of defeat.

God remains busily at work in the midst of our bad choices and the resulting suffering. God's circumstantial will is activated within the evil, working in the direction of salvaging the intentional will. God's circumstantial will has great meaning and effect. It opens the way to God's ultimate triumph with no loss of anything of value to ourselves in the final analysis. No evil circumstance can ever befall us that can stop us from finding in it, through God's gracious help, a path along which God's intended will can still be realized.

3. **God's Ultimate Will.** Persuasive love, as opposed to reverting to coercion, is how God typically achieves divine intentions in the face of bad human choices. God works in all things toward the good of those whom he loves (Rom 8:28). Weatherhead insists that God's intentional goal will ultimately will be achieved through one route or another, and in spite of any and all frustrations and sufferings we have caused in the meantime. "That is what I mean by God's omnipotence—not that everything that happens is his will, but that nothing can happen which finally defeats his will."

The cross of Jesus is a prime example. God never intended that Jesus should die brutally. The intention was that the life and teachings of Jesus would have swayed the crowds and religious establishment toward accepting the arriving kingdom of love. Human choice went the other way. Therefore, the circumstantial will of God, God's will in the circumstances that human evil created, was as follows: Jesus should accept death in a positive and redemptive way that could lead eventually to God's ultimate will, the redemption of sinning humanity.[32]

> God adapts the strategy for accomplishing divine intentions, working creatively in evil circumstances of our own making.

Jesus made possible a way back to God by using the cross, born of human sin, as an instrument to reach the goal of God's ultimate will. We who are willing to follow Jesus are called to do the same in our present circumstances. We are to carry our crosses and accept God's loving enablement for finding ways of enduring suffering and redirecting evil toward God's ultimate goal. Weatherhead concludes with this:

> Rest in this thought about God's ultimate will. "Eye hath not seen, nor ear heard, neither have entered into the heart of man, the things which God hath prepared for them that love him." Trust God. Rest in the nature of God. He who began this strange adventure we call human life will also control the end. "I am Alpha and Omega, the beginning and the end, the first and the last."

Even Jesus, the obedient Son of God, cried in the face of our sin-caused circumstances (see chapter six). So will we if we follow him faithfully. And, like him, we also can be instruments of God's redemption of present circumstances in the service of God's ultimate will.

But there's more than our following faithfully and sometimes blindly through periods of pain. There is this wonderful assurance. Along the jagged way, we can be sure that the God "who began a good work in you will carry it on to completing until the day of Jesus Christ" (Phil 1:6).

A Holy Walking

The threefold dimensions of the will of God bring us to this bottom line. God's intentional will is clear and, despite intervening circumstances, God's ultimate will is assured. In the meantime, God's grace is sufficient. God's power is disciplined by the divine love and is perfected even in our weakness. When we are weak, then are we strong. "As much as sin may abound, God's grace abounds even more" (Rom 5:20).

That's Paul's 8-9-10 pathway witness and the keynote for Christian life in this world. It reflects perfectly the O-D-R understanding of our faith walk as seen in the Psalms. It also tracks well with the journey of Jesus as his path went from life and teaching (orientation) to brutal death (disorientation) to dramatic resurrection (reorientation).

The Christian pathway travels from our thorns in the flesh to our opportunities to be in the third heaven with Paul. It shouts that in every cold tomb life lies waiting to burst forth! It drips in victory even when explanations about lingering death are still lacking. It must walk by faith, to be sure, but it's a holy walking guided by the Holy One and headed toward a holy goal.

How do we survive and even flourish in the Christian life, especially in the face of the worst that may come along? We do it by taking the stuff of our ordinary lives, our parents and children, our spouses and friends, our workplaces and fellow workers, our dreams and fantasies, our attachments and temptations, our easily accessible gratifications, our depersonalizing of intimate relations, and "placing it all on the altar of refining fire—our God is a consuming fire—and finding it all stuff redeemed for a life of holiness."[33]

Exploring the several dimensions of the 8-9-10 path will help humble disciples of Jesus walk through the thorns and on to the glories. Pain may even increase when we believe since, by imitating Jesus, we will accept the pain of others as our own and draw wholly undeserved persecution. Some mystery will remain since we will not be able to explain from what lair the snake came to Adam and Eve or why particular events happen or don't happen when we live faithfully and pray in faith believing.

No matter. We will learn to live in the mystery and function in the tension. We will be comforted in knowing that, wherever the snake came from and whatever mischief it now manages to create, its head is already cut off! We will learn to live under the cloud of not knowing the answers to some of our perplexing questions about suffering and evil. The following will be enough. The resurrection of Jesus assures us that God is alive and by our side. One day the answers will come. Pain has its limits and, in fact, already is defeated. We now live and walk in hope "that the creation itself will be set free from its bondage to decay and will obtain the freedom of the glory of the children of God" (Rom 8:21).

With that amazing assurance always in mind, I proceed to the following chapters. I begin with the burden, the hard questions, the problem of pain. From there I will work my way down the jagged pathway of faith and finally arrive at the goal, the eternal glory. That's the basic map of the jagged journey of Christian faith. It accepts the New Testament witness that Jesus, having lived, died, and been raised to new life, is the dawning of a new age. He is "the Way" (John 14:6), the path, the route of our faith journey. As we travel with the Master, we will hurt, rejoice, learn, love, and always worship. If faithful, we will carry our own crosses, be sources of healing for many who hurt, and one day experience our own resurrection.

The Christian's jagged journey is the Bible's big picture of reality. While it includes suffering, it is much more. It's more than the deterioration and dying of frail bodies common to all humans. It includes, in fact features a cross in the heart of God and only then a cross jammed into a hill outside Jerusalem. It's also our sacred calling to choose the carrying of our own cross in this world as an extension of the suffering of Jesus. By living in our frail humanity as Jesus lived in the flesh, we will be fruitful in our service to others and finally saved ourselves.

The history of the church is filled with saints, martyrs, and the mass of unknown faithful who have faced this world courageously and joyously, with all its good and bad. They came to know something wonderful as they lived this instruction of Psalm 34: "I bless God every chance I get; my lungs expand with his praise; I live and breathe God." Note that this psalm includes "when things aren't going well." Life in Christ hardly intends to lift us out of the world of the mundane and broken. To the contrary, we are ushered deeper into it. Jesus sought out the lost, sick, and lonely and marvelously ministered to them.

To be eligible for God's help, all one has to do is be in trouble for the sake of Christ. To be faithful to the helping God, we must step into trouble with gratitude on our lips. And it's precisely in the messiness and painfulness of life in the raw that a wonderful truth is found. Psalm 34:18 reports that "if your heart is broken, you'll find God right there; if you're kicked in the gut, he'll help you catch your breath." We are further assured that "God keeps an eye on his friends, his ears pick up every moan and groan" (vs. 15).

Upon my leaving seminary, our president addressed my class with this shocking statement. "I hope for you all this one thing. After the first ten years in ministry, I hope you will be able to report ten failures you've experienced, five scars you've acquired, and numerous tears you've shed. If you can report this, I'll know that you've been on the road with Jesus, risking all, fearing nothing, giving yourself away, sharing his ministry that leads to a cross—and an empty tomb!" That's wisdom learned by the faithful over the centuries. That's the voice of the Bible. That's the holy walking of true saints of God.

WE SAY

Take it Away!
(2 Cor 12:8)

4

BURDEN OF THE MYSTERY

With Things This Way, Can God Really Exist?

If God were good, he would wish to make his creatures perfectly happy, and if God were almighty he would be able to do what he wished. But the creatures are not happy. Therefore, God lacks either goodness, or power, or both. This is the problem of pain in its simplest form.[34]

Pain plunges like a sword through creation.[35] Then Job's wife said to him, "Curse God and die!" (Job 2:9). Prayed a frustrated prophet to God, "Let me put my case to you. Why does the way of the guilty prosper? Why do all who are treacherous thrive?" (Jer 12:1).

Blaming ourselves or even God for various evils in our lives or in this world is usually a faulty and fruitless exercise. But, since real problems remain and cry out for explanation, we continue to do it. Knowing that God works through love more than by wielding sheer power helps us understand and cope with our miseries, even find hope for turning them into positives. But it does it take away entirely the mystery and burden of having to suffer in God's world.

We wish things were simpler, cleaner, and fairer, but they aren't. Life comes at us like a jumble of oddities and paradoxes, dilemmas and hard decisions, justices and injustices, surprises and shocks, bits of joy and bursts of pain and loss. Where in all of this is the good order, consistent love, and full control of a sovereign and loving God?

Take the horrific Great Lisbon earthquake of 1755. It's estimated to have been as severe as 9.0 on the Richter scale, with the death toll in Lisbon, Portugal, about one-quarter of the population of 200,000, and many of the city's great structures flattened. Tsunamis as tall as sixty feet swept the coast of North Africa killing thousands. They reached Greenland and are claimed to have struck Martinique and Barbados clear across the Atlantic Ocean.

This event was a turning point of our modern era. It happened on All Saints Day. Was it God's harsh judgment on wayward humans? Was it only that time's typical way of reading such otherwise unexplainable events? It certainly impacted the Age of Enlightenment (so much for a naïve optimism). It stimulated a fresh wave of atheism and represented the beginnings of seismology since scientific explanations were sought by some. John and Charles Wesley in England engaged the subject by arguing for a constructive marriage of faith and reason.[36]

When the unspeakable happens, what is the explanation? Need we choose between faith and reason? Can God work through "natural" events? Does evil now have a life of its own in this fallen world, with God temporarily taking hands off? Was God, disengaged, disinterested, or not present at all?

Shouldn't It Be Different?

Surely such awful things shouldn't happen in the world of a good and all-powerful God. Or does God not exist? Or does God, good or not, sometimes strike out viciously in righteous anger? Or is the whole thing too much for us to ever understand? Why should innocent people suffer? Why do guilty people seem to escape suffering? We, even we who believe in God, appear to live in a world full of unchecked dangers and unanswered questions.

Mystery persists as a major burden we Christians are forced to carry. I'm hurting and trying to believe, so why doesn't God take away the pain? Shakespeare put this in the mouth of Macduff: "Each new morn, new widows howl, new orphans cry, new sorrows strike heaven on the face."[37] Our daily news reports are full of genocide, terrorism, traffic deaths, abuse of children, fraud in high places, etc. That's just how it is. But why?

In reacting to suffering, even we who believe in Jesus are tempted to minimize it, deny it, try hard to look the other way, wonder why we aren't exempt. We easily slip into the thinking of the fallen culture around us, moving quickly to defend whatever comfort and stability we still have. We shift the blame wherever we can.

"Not me." "Not now." "It's not that bad." "It'll go away quickly." "I'll get a facelift, buy insurance, hire security people, buy a gun, move to a better neighborhood, take the newest pill, pray harder until God finally takes it from me." But trouble comes anyway and sometimes refuses to go away. Why? Some come to a harsh conclusion. Either God should take better care of us or we should be done with the whole God business.

Statue at Gethsemani monastery in Kentucky, in honor of Jonathan Daniels, seminarian martyred in Alabama, 1965, advocating for civil rights.

I wrote these lines on my seventy-fifth birthday while sitting in a little coffee shop with the warm morning sun flooding in the window. It was an ironic scene, me being relaxed and comfortable while writing about suffering. But the irony didn't last long. The call came. A good friend had just died. I didn't want to hear it, but there was no choice. There's no place to hide, not even in a cozy little coffee shop. That's a glimpse of the jagged journey, a lovely breakfast setting and a sudden death, all in the same morning.

On that eventful morning I was in good health as far as I knew. My car was sitting outside with its odometer reading a mere 2,777 miles. It was new, paid for, and the 777 in the number of miles made me think of a tripling of the perfect Hebrew number 7. Beauty, privilege, peace. What a wonderful morning it was—before the call, of course. It's always before...

On the other hand, it wasn't just that sudden death. It had been a terrible week in the country. Two police shootings of young black males in Louisiana and Minnesota had resulted in a sniper in Texas killing five police officers. Just the day before I had been driving near my home to visit the family of a deceased Christian from Haiti, a land so full of pain. Suddenly I encountered on the road ahead by what appeared to be a wild turkey. It actually was a vulture picking up a dead squirrel and flying away for a great lunch of fresh carrion. A car, not mine, had probably killed the little animal that now was nothing more than meat to support the next level of the food chain.

So goes life in our troubled world. Where will faith go when it's based on the assumption of a truly good and all-powerful God who, nonetheless, doesn't right the many wrongs? Shouldn't things be different than this? Can we really believe when they aren't different?

Does God Have ADHD?

My wife and I recently saw the 2017 movie version of *Beauty and the Beast*. It makes so clear that appearances can mask reality. Beautiful and beastly, just and very unjust, pleasure and pain. Where's the actual reality? If God is good and all-powerful, surely things would be different, more according to the divine intent. But they aren't. We're left with the burdensome mystery of why many things are as they are. Faith seems always under attack.

> Is God remote from our real lives, not hearing our pain and pleadings, doing nothing but being his perfect self?

Have circumstances ever led you to think of God as suffering from ADHD (Attention Deficit Hyperactive Disorder)? The psalmist certainly did. He reports this frustrated prayer thrown at God: "Please, pay attention!" (Ps 5:1). It was not enough that God had been hyperactive in the past—creating worlds, a people, routing enemies, etc. Right now, when the psalmist was in trouble, God apparently was distracted and having trouble focusing on the situation at hand. The divine ears were deaf and the powerful hands inactive.

The palmist was begging God to wake up, focus, act to fix a badly broken world. "Please pay attention to me now, activate your hyperactive capacities, show up and do something! I may be rambling, groaning, crying irrationally, but surely you can see through all that." God is reported to have "a reputation for welcoming God-seekers" (5:12). So why is there no living up to the divine reputation when help is needed so badly?

With enemies at the door and pain piling up, why was God so silent? Had deafness been added to God's ADHD? How long will it be necessary to wait for any kind of response? We humans are caught between Psalm 8 and 13. First, we marvel at the greatness of God and the creation and naturally ask, "Why do you bother with us?" (8:4). Then we suffer, get frustrated at the Divine's silence, and complain, "Long enough, God—you've ignored me long enough!" (13:1). According to a Yiddish proverb, "God will provide, but, oh that he would until he finally does!"

Here's the constant question. Is God real and available? If real and not responsive, is God somehow disabled and no longer capable of changing things when I really hurt? Will the divine power be employed on my behalf when things go bad? When jolted by life's jagged journey, will God be there, actively caring, comforting, healing, adequate for the worst we face? Will we know the answer until we get there? The words of C. S. Lewis that head this chapter are disturbing. Could the problem of my pain spell the end of God, at least no God for me when I'm hurting so intensely?

> Suffering and evil present a challenge to any faith in an all-powerful God whose heart supposedly is love.

The experience of Ruby Sales is common, even if it appears in different forms in different places and times. Ruby is an African American woman who grew up a Baptist in the South and was steeped in what she has called "black folk religion." She became a civil rights activist, sure that God was totally on her side. When the police horses surrounded her, blocking her access to the all-white restrooms, she expected God to intervene, repeating the Exodus miracle, opening a path in the equine wall that would lead directly to free-access bathrooms and the promised land of justice for all.

But it didn't happen. Ruby was shocked, wondering how God could be so calloused, so wrong when the cause was clearly so right. She became a Marxist and materialist on the spot! That began her now-celebrated journey to recover a socially relevant faith and a public theology that could undergird the deep spiritual needs of today's American population. She had been faced with an apparently stark reality. With things as they are, apparently God *isn't* or *can't* or for some inexcusable reason *won't*.

Can God be counted on when it hurts, when things are so unjust? Seemingly not, at least in the experience of many. The disillusioned identify with a vivid passage in Carlyle's book *Sartor Resqrtus*. It pictures a man gazing down at midnight from his high attic window. He sees shadowy city streets where thousands are herded together or isolated and alone, people dying and others being born, some singing and others cursing. He sits above it all, alone with the stars above and a mass of confusion, merriment, and misery below.

Is God like that, high above, remote from our real lives, not even hearing our pain and pleadings, doing nothing but being the ultimate of perfection? Might the relative insignificance of our little lives our lives slip on past God, being no more than Disraeli's philosophy of life, "youth is a blunder, manhood a struggle, old age a regret." Is the writer of Ecclesiastes right in saying, "vanity of vanities, all is vanity!"?[38]

Apparently yes, but not necessarily. We likely all have heard the classic words sung so often in presentations of *Carousel*:

> When you walk through a storm
> Keep your head up high
> And don't be afraid of the dark.
> At the end of the storm is a golden sky
> And the sweet silver song of a lark.
>
> Walk on through the wind,
> Walk on through the rain,
> Tho' your dreams be tossed and blown.
> Walk on, Walk on, with hope in your heart
> And you'll never walk alone,
> You'll never walk alone.

Yes, we've heard and been moved by those lovely words. But what if they're only the romantic stuff of musical theater? What if present indications are that you are walking alone? Friends have proven fickle and apparently God is on an extended vacation with his smart phone out of range. That's when suffering really hurts! We must walk on through wind and rain, but it seems that we are walking alone with no destination in sight.

A Thin Red Line

C. S. Lewis once wrote a whole chapter on "animal pain." He reports that "so far as we know beasts are incapable of either sin or virtue, therefore they can neither deserve or be improved by it."[39] Apparently the animal world is just tooth and claw, kill or be killed, live as best you can until something kills you for its lunch or dinner. In a world without sin or virtue, nothing is gained or lost. But what about the world of humans?

In his early days Lewis was an atheist and never would have been tempted to refer to the violent world of nature to prove the existence of God, certainly not a good God. After all, the vast majority of our universe is dark, empty, and extremely cold. On the rare place called Earth, life manages to exist, but most of the time the living beings, even human beings, are busy preying on each other. The creatures cause pain by being born, live by inflicting pain, and mostly die in pain. Does that suggest a gracious God to you?

Humans, observes Lewis, are much the same as the animal world, and we have an additional problem. We can reason, foresee our own coming death, and suffer the deepest of anguish since we desire a permanence that clearly is impossible. So, concludes Lewis, this atheist who later became a devoted Christian, "if the universe is so bad, or even half so bad, how on earth did human beings ever come to attribute it to the activity of a wise and good Creator?"[40] Good question. Lewis elsewhere explains his own surprising journey to Christian faith,[41] but first things first.

We must feel the weight of the burden before suggesting a solution. Suffering is a great challenge to any faith in an all-powerful God whose heart supposedly is love. *Providence* is the usual word for the way God acts to promote the well-being of humans and all creation. Given the ungodly chaos of evil and injustice so prominent in this world, it's natural for us to wonder if God is truly powerful, really good, actually in control, even real. Providence is a problem.

Theological models of how God acts run from mystery (we just don't and probably can't know), to full control (all happens according to God's precise plan), to relational love (God's love grants freedom to creatures and then works mostly through the promptings of love, not manipulative control of people and events).[42] These are only models of divine providence, and widely diverse ones at that. But one has to choose and the choice affects the rest of our theological thinking. Each model is able to be supported by select biblical passages. Especially when pressured by life's experiences of suffering, I judge that the relational-love model emerges as most convincing and satisfying.[43]

Lines from two movies make the burden and challenge clear. *The Thin Red Line* intersperses haunting voice-overs with awful World War II battle scenes of the fight to control the South Pacific island of Guadalcanal. The voice is of a young soldier pondering the "thin red line" of war that separates life and death. "This great evil. Where's it come from? Who's doing this? Who's killing us? Does our ruin benefit the Earth? Does it help the grass to grow or the sun to shine? Is this darkness in you [God] too? Have you passed through the night?"

It's hard to pass through the night of great suffering and not ask such questions about the frailty of life, the sinfulness of ourselves, the awful brutality of war, and even the questionable existence of God. The greatest single question of the religious life likely is this: "If I call out to God, will anyone answer?" This heavy question brings to mind the second movie, *From Dusk Till Dawn*.

Two criminals and their hostages unknowingly seek temporary refuge in an establishment populated by vampires, with chaotic results. I don't recommend all this violence and vampires, except for one thing. This movie also features a pastor who had lost his faith. At one point his daughter says to him, "Daddy, don't you believe in God anymore?" His response is painful: "Every person who chooses the service of God as his life's work has something in common. I don't care if you're a preacher, a priest, a nun, a rabbi, or a Buddhist monk. Many, many times during your life you will look in a mirror and ask yourself: 'Am I a fool?'"

There it is, cold and unwelcome but common and real. Our religion is a matter of faith, maybe reasonable and reassured faith much of the time, but still faith that is subject to haunting wonderings, especially in times of trial.

We see this problem in the Bible. Job 14 is a common Bible reading for Holy Saturday, that awkward day between the horror of crucifixion Friday and the wonder of resurrection Sunday. It's the day that haunts our fragile human lives. It's the time of our waiting anxiously between two worlds, the one of darkness, death, and despair and the one of blazing new light when eternal life, it is hoped, finally will burst onto our troubled scene.

This passage in Job begins by reporting that our living is for only a few days, and they tend to be filled with trouble. It ends with a haunting question tinged with at least a hint of hope. "If mortals die, will they live again?" That's the perennial question. We hurt and hope. We live with the mystery of things that are not welcome and have no easy explanations. We join the biblical prophets in crying out to God, "How long?" Will anyone answer?

This urgent cry is heard in several of the psalms. It's echoed by Jeremiah and then Habakkuk, who broods over the apparent dumbness of God in the face of intolerable injustices. "How many times do I have to yell 'Help!'? . . . The wicked have the righteous hamstrung and stand justice on its head" (Hab 1:1–4). Even the martyrs in heaven blurt out this same painful question. How long will spilled blood go unrevenged? (Rev 6:9–10). If God doesn't act, maybe the divine can't see, hear, isn't able to do anything about the problem, or maybe doesn't exist in the first place. That's the mystery, the unknown, the burden we must carry when we hurt and our prayers seem to hang helplessly in the air.

If God is really there and truly loving, and with evil and suffering loose in God's world, how can God not be directly responsible for their presence? Who can blame the many Jews who, during their ancient Exile and modern Holocaust, gave up on God? How can God be sovereign in the heights and also inactive in the valleys where things go very wrong? It's the perennial question of God and evil. It's the challenge of our faith.

5

GOD AND EVIL

Isn't Evil and Injustice God's Own Fault?

Eve and Adam made their fateful choices in the garden, so they are truly responsible. And yet, they didn't create the snake or their own ability, even their inclination to choose wrongly. So who did? Dare we accuse God?

The big word is "providence," the ways God acts to promote our human well-being and that of all creation. What are those ways, especially in the face of awful evil? Can this be it? "Freely given love is so important to God that he allows our planet to be a cancer of evil in his universe—for a time."

—Philip Yancey, *Where Is God When It Hurts?*

Is there life after death, joy after pain, a payoff for all our hoping and believing? Those are big and persistent questions. And here's another, one that suffering and abused people tend to bring up all the time. Is the God of the *hills* also the God of the *valleys*? Is the God of a good creation also still truly God when that creation is spoiled? If so, is God always sovereign, actually in control? If God is in control, how can evil rage unchecked?

It's impossible for a rational person to love and worship a God who is responsible for evil. But what if God's very nature is love and God chooses not to coerce but allow evil if that is our perverted choice? Would evil then be God's responsibility or ours? What of Philip Yancey's comment above? Is the cancer of evil that's seeming to run our world allowed to exist because God is so committed to love? Can God be truly loving and allow evil to rage unchecked?

Hills and Valleys

The geographic question about hills and valleys is dramatized in 1 Kings 20. The story is told of the king of Syria tragically making a wrong assumption. The Jews and their God, so he thought, belonged to the hills where they had enjoyed a series of military victories. But in the valleys, down low and separated from their God, they would be sitting ducks just waiting to be slaughtered. So the Jews were lured to the plains and the big battle followed.

The result? Tragedy for Syria whose king had supposed the wrong thing. The fact was (is) that the mountain-God is also the plains-God! Geography presents no divine limitation. God is also present on the low ground, suffering in the dirt with us and prepared to bring us victory. But God suffering? How can that be if God is God? How powerful is evil? How weak is God? Is suffering the same thing as weakness?

The great Scottish preacher James Stewart speaks eloquently about this story. He applies it to our pressing human needs. "The God of our joys is the God of our sorrows too. . . . The God of our great religious experiences is the God of our common days as well. . . . The God of life's sunlit heights is also the God of the last and deepest and darkest valley of all, the valley of the shadow of death."[44] But the hard question stands. If God is sovereign on the heights and in the plains, why is there so much unchecked evil?

Not far from the boyhood town of Nazareth that Jesus knew so well were two other little towns close together, Cana and Nain. The New Testament reports a wedding in one and a funeral in the other, with Jesus *present at both!* That divine presence in the ups and downs of life is a comforting thought. Even so, it's hard to embrace the comfort when pain and fear and grief slam into us. When we humans face the tragic and unexplainable, getting lost in the darkness of circumstance or ravaged by some awful disease, we tend to expect God to do more than just be there. We want God to *act*, change things, rout the enemy, and clear up the mysteries and frightening unknowns.

If God does not act, does that put God at fault? Have you ever prayed this: "Dear Lord, make the bad go away and answer my urgent questions with more than delays and riddles or my death will be your doing." If not, you still may. So many others have. They expect the divine presence to make a divine difference. A dramatic example happened on the Sea of Galilee.

The disciples were glad they had Jesus in the boat with them, but why would he just sleep at their feet when they were thrashing in frantic fear? After all, they were doing what he had suggested. "Let us go over to the other side" (Mark 4:35). They had set out to cross the Sea during the night, something against their better judgment. Jesus had seemed relaxed about it, so they had reluctantly agreed. Now they were facing death from a terrible storm.

Admittedly, Jesus hadn't said, "Sail with me and I'll guarantee smooth seas all the way." But they didn't expect all of this! When tragedy was closing in, Jesus was sleeping quietly. Did he also have a touch of ADHD like sometimes seems to affect his Father (see chapter four). Was he having a pleasant dream and failing to focus on the crisis at hand?

Having sailed on the highs of faith, the disciples now were diving into the lows from which they might not return.

> The cancer of evil seems to be running our world. How can a God of love allow this to rage unchecked?

Who could blame them for blurting out, "Jesus, wake up! You got us into this mess, now get us out!" We who suffer don't have the privilege of jumping straight from the cross to Easter Sunday, skipping quickly from the Saturday of hurting and wondering to the resurrection we were promised would come. We see the waves rolling around us and are on the edge of being overwhelmed by the mysteries of evil and suffering. If Jesus doesn't come out of that tomb and we also perish, won't God be at fault?

Then there were the two men walking on the road to Emmaus. They had so hoped in Jesus, and now he was dead. It had been a wonderful but failed mirage. Jesus had been a beautiful vision that became mired hopelessly in this earth's ugliness. The earlier faith of these men in the supposed Messiah had brought strength and direction to life, and then soured badly when injustice crashed in and idealisms crumbled. Dead and humiliated on a Roman cross, the living water and bread of life, as Jesus had referred to himself, were now dried up in an evil sun and picked over by the vultures of this world. Thought these two devastated men on the road, "We were fools to have sacrificed so much—and all for nothing!"

Wonderful words of only a few days back had become twisted in their minds. Maybe what Jesus had really said was, "If anyone thirst, come to me and you might thirst worse than ever!" The high hills of hope were now the deep valleys of despair. Was there any real meaning to those shining words from the prophet: "For waters shall break forth in the wilderness, and streams in the desert; the burning sand shall become a pool, and the thirsty ground springs of water" (Isa 35:6–7)? How easily people can be tricked and die in the desert!

Many would rather perish at the hands of mindless fate than at the hands of a loving God failing to love in the time of crisis. At best, we struggling humans seem to live in a perpetual Advent. That's the season of the Christian year that waits patiently for the Christmas birth. The coming of Jesus is promised but not yet here. We hope but still hurt, are anxious and tempted to doubt. The prophet announces that the Lord's house will be built on the highest mountain. It will be seen by all the nations, a global magnet of goodness and joy (Isa 2:1–5). Our problem is that it's not here, not yet—maybe never?

We're still stuck in the deep valleys of sorrow, frustration, loss, and danger. We're distracted by our immediate circumstances. We're still low, very low, often in the muck of our own making. The divine heights seem so unreal, so unreachable. Has God died or fallen asleep? Can God do nothing about the evil, or for some strange reason will God do nothing about it?

Here's an answer that deserves consideration, one that will be considered later in this chapter. God's very nature is uncontrolling love. Creaturely free will is a genuine reality, a divine gift. God is not an all-directing dictator. God "never controls others but calls all creation toward love and beauty."[45] God indeed is in every valley of ours, nudging everything and everyone toward the good. But for now God does not control all things by sheer force but works lovingly within and even through all things on behalf of the good (Rom 8:28).

Jesus gave his disciples a warning and a promise. The warning was that they must not pretend to be doing good as a public show, calling attention to themselves. If they do, God won't be applauding. The promise? If the good is done quietly, with no personal credit being sought, disciples will be acting as God typically does, lovingly "working behind the scenes" on their behalf (Matt 6:4). The work may not be obvious or the results immediate, but it's never work done in vain.

We don't find in the Bible a flurry of divine executive orders ensuring that God's will is always done precisely as planned. History is not a printout of preprogrammed events. It's open and dynamic, with we creatures joining

God in its writing. Maybe we're the ones at fault when evil temporarily prevails. Maybe Paul is right. While God can do anything, more than we "could ever imagine or guess or request," God chooses not to do it "by pushing us around but by working within us, his Spirit deeply and gently within us" (Eph 3:20–21).

The natural outflow of the divine heart, the preferred manner of God's working, is not the glare of coercive power but more the delicate pastels, the soft yellows and gentle greens, the sweetness of sacrificial love. When looking toward God in light of Jesus and inspired by the Spirit, God's primary color tends to be a rainbow dominated with the hues of holy love (1 John 4:8; Eph 3:17–18).[46]

After the Fire

We're glad when a preacher announces that God is with us in the good and bad times. Maybe, however, that's just too easy an announcement, not the whole story. Mother Teresa reported one day that she had met a lady who was dying of cancer. She told her, "You know, this terrible pain is only the kiss of Jesus—a sign that you have come so close to Jesus on the cross that he can kiss you." As they joined hands together, the woman responded, "Mother Teresa, please tell Jesus to stop kissing me." Dismissing pain with a glib even if well-meant comment rarely helps, even if it comes from a beloved Roman Catholic saint.

My first novel was about submarine warfare in World War II. I picture a scene of devastation after a sea battle. Were there really any winners? Left behind was mostly a trail of sorrow crying out for future revenge. Violence can bring a kind of peace, but only temporarily. It also brings pain and loss that elude adequate description. No shallow words will make them go away.

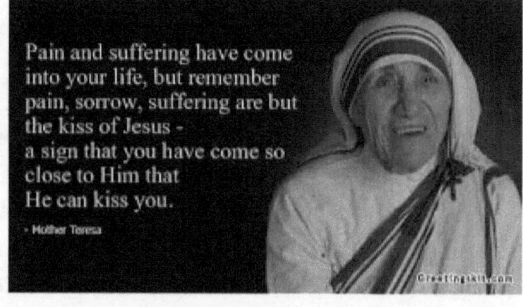

Pain and suffering have come into your life, but remember pain, sorrow, suffering are but the kiss of Jesus - a sign that you have come so close to Him that He can kiss you.
- Mother Teresa

I describe what this submarine had violently deposited on the water's surface with its well-aimed torpedo. "The gentle light of the moon was dancing on the ripples of the deep, normally a romantic scene that now was twisted toward the revolting. . . . The wreckage of the destroyer cried back at the sky, seeming to scream out very hard questions. When will we get our chance to get even? Had anyone won this day's conflict? Were those still alive a little less so than before? Was God watching, caring, or voluntarily absent from such an awful scene?"[47]

Elie Wiesel speaks in similar ways from the war's devastation that he witnessed on land in Europe. His slim volume reeks of the terrifying madness of war that had erupted in history and now resides in the troubled conscience of humankind. He writes so that we won't forget, which would be giving the enemy one more victory, killing the dead a second time. He pictures a horrible scene in the Nazi death camp of Auschwitz. A young Jewish man is hanged cruelly for some minor infraction of a camp rule. His body dangles limply, displayed for all other prisoners to stare at. Millions of other Jews met similar senseless fates.

Someone asked prisoner Wiesel, "Where is God now?" Here was his devastating response. "Where is He? Here He is—He is hanging here on this gallows!"[48] Psalm 22 and Job 23 are likewise dark. Something wild and ugly is loose in this world. Evil, injustice, and suffering are everywhere. They are no respecter of persons, worshippers of God or not. Is God also a victim, or at least our ability to believe in him? Can God stop the evil? If the answer is yes, then why hasn't the evil been stopped? Did God once exist and now is hanging helplessly at the hands of this world's madness?

There were at least two options available to God's people after the firestorm of such radical injustice. Wiesel lost faith in God and refused to forget or forgive. Corrie Ten Boom chose differently. She also had suffered in a Nazi death camp and survived with this testimony. "Some questions remain, but they are not to be feared. Our heavenly father holds all things in His hands, even our questions. With Jesus, even in our darkest moments, the best remains. And the very best is yet to be."[49] The biblical prophet Habakkuk, having questioned God in great frustration, also ended up with "yet will I rejoice in the Lord" (Hab 3:17–18). When we get no answers from God, we still can know his character and rely on his heart.

How we wish that our faith communities could rise above the waves of evil, that God would answer all questions and stamp out all pain and injustice. Bertrand Russell troubles us when he recalls that Christian church history brings little encouragement. The more the intensity of religious commitment the greater has been the worldly state of affairs. There was the Christian-initiated Inquisition with all its tortures and the many women burned as witches.[50] Will we humans ever get it right? Is God able but unwilling to do something about the mess we're in and the messes we create?

Maybe we're not seeing all that's there. Where is God during and after the fire? Is God absent or are we just blind? If God could have prevented the devastation and did not, is God really good? Or is God so good, so loving, that evil sometimes will prevail, at least for now, when humans with free will make awful choices?

I'll say it right out. It may be that God cannot unilaterally prevent all evil. When a loving God is defied, the evil creature is to blame, not God. John Wesley has it right. God's power should be understood more in terms of empowerment than over-powerment. If true, this distinction is very important. It explains who God really is and where our hope lies

Even When God Is Silent

It's always been the case. We face forward in faith and yet are frustrated over the silence and apparent inactivity of God, especially in times of pain. The early Christians in Corinth apparently had the same needs and confusions as we do. Paul told them, "the Jews require a sign and the Greeks seek after wisdom" (1 Cor 1:22). One group wanted a divine action to change the circumstance and the other sought an intellectually satisfying explanation of the circumstance.

When things go wrong, we want them changed and answers to our "why" questions. Why did this happen to me? How difficult it is when we pray, "God, do something quickly!" and there comes silence from the heavens.

We are all Jews and Greeks. We want action and answers. The problem in ancient Corinth and still where we live is that divine action often fails to come right after our prayer, and answers to the tough questions don't usually fall out of the sky just because we want them. The needed actions and explanations rarely appear precisely how and exactly when we wish, if at all. That's part of our pain and suffering as fallen humans. It's part of our confusion about God.

Days grind on without an answer. The psalmist says, "I run to you, God; I run for dear life. Don't let me down! Take me seriously this time! . . . I've cried my eyes out; I feel hollow inside. My life leaks away, groan by groan; my years fade out in sighs" (Ps 31). Faith still remains, but its strained by lack of fulfillment. Our hearts keep reaching, but soon they struggle with doubt and even verge on despair.

Paul tells the Corinthians something helpful. God does provide an enduring answer to our cries, and it's the same one received by the Jews and Greeks long ago. It's not the answer expected or commonly accepted. No matter, it's God's response. The answer to the questions raised by human suffering is *a dramatic display of God's suffering!*

According to Paul, we are to preach *Christ crucified*, an obstacle to some and foolishness to others. The Jews wanted a warrior king who would ride in majesty and vindicate his people by eliminating the pain. The Greeks wanted a rational explanation to remove the mysteries of life and found Paul's answer sheer absurdity, a worsening of the confusion. The wisdom found in the cross of Jesus doesn't compute for the "worldly." Jesus told his disciples to follow him to death if they wanted to find life. At best, this is an odd and unwelcome instruction. Nevertheless, the truth lies with this reversal of usual wisdom. The relief of our pain is tied to the pain of God. The Eternal One who lives forever once died for us!

We must reframe our questions, change our expectations, rethink who God is and how God works in this fallen world.[51] Our faith, if it's to survive, must take this in or risk its own demise. All Christian roads will be jagged and not always lead to an immediate "miraculous" action of God on our behalf. Instead, they all will lead *to Calvary*. Our pain will be resolved only in the light of God's pain and patience. Jesus died because of our bad choices that hurt ourselves and others. "In Christ, we don't find a God who is 'strong enough' to overthrow powers and principalities by force. In Christ, we find a God who is strong enough to practice radical solidarity. In Christ, God suffers."[52]

This central truth is hardly about the weakness of God—surely there's no lack of the Creator's ability to act decisively. It's about two things. First, God created humans with the ability to choose the intended good. Second, the great love of God accepts our decisions and is open to participating constructively in the suffering created by the evil of our wrong choices. Our suffering must be viewed in light of God's great love and voluntary vulnerability on our behalf. Our ability to choose is a gift of God, a "risk" God has willingly and lovingly taken. This divine love and vulnerability are seen most clearly in a barn near Bethlehem and on a cross near Jerusalem.

A friend of mine often takes groups of Americans to various African countries to experience the worst of the worst, the plight of AIDS orphans.

He says to the teams before they go: "It's 90 percent presence and 10 percent performance." Just choosing to be there speaks more loudly to the desperate young Africans than the little bit of building or painting or teaching that comparatively rich Americans can manage while there.

God obviously agrees. The divine decision about our human plight was not to send us a check. No, God came *personally*, put the heavenly person on the line, *enfleshed* reaching love, was tempted, suffered, and murdered. God absorbed pain in order that we might know the truth of his love and find the way to truly live, now and eternally.

The wonderful news is that God both *is* and is *open* to us faltering, failing, and hurting humans. God is not remote, removed, untouched by our infirmities, pains, and injustices. God reaches. But more, God comes, especially in Jesus, and willingly bore the brunt of evil on his own back. Quietly, powerfully, and sweetly, God has made of that cross of Jesus a saving instrument that draws the world toward repentance and God's saving love and intentional will.

> God provides an answer to our cries. The divine answer to our suffering is a dramatic display of God's suffering!

Is evil God's own fault? Regardless of appearances to the contrary, the answer is "no!" God is not responsible for the rampant evil on this earth, nor is God out of touch with it or inactive toward it. We can say that God made evil *possible*, the risk involved in loving and granting freedom to us so that we could love in return (or not love). We humans are the ones who make evil *actual*. We do it by our chosen violation of intended loving relationships with God and each other. That is why God came and Jesus cried. Yes, Jesus, God-with-us, cried.

6

EVEN JESUS CRIED

Can God Suffer and Still Be God?

Then he began to teach them that the Son of Man must undergo great suffering, and be rejected by the elders, the chief priests, and the scribes, and be killed, and after three days rise again. . . . He called the crowd with his disciples, and said to them, "If any want to become my followers, let them deny themselves and take up their cross and follow me" (Mark 31–34, NRSV).

Jesus experienced God-forsakenness on the cross when he cried out, "My God, my God! Why have you forsaken me?" Here we see the ultimate strength—a God strong enough to voluntarily become weak and plunge into vulnerability and darkness out of love for us. And here we see the greatest possible glory—the willingness to lay aside all his glory out of love for us.[53]

I don't know how to put this gently, so I'll say it directly. At least by usual standards of this world, Jesus ranged somewhere between unbelievable and downright stupid. He came to this world with every advantage by being equal with God. He had the power to accomplish everything he wished. And what did he do? He threw in the towel, defaulted, gave up his great advantage, called it quits, cried like every other baby. He voluntarily submitted to suffering, even of the worst kind (Phil 2:5–8).

Isn't that as poor a performance as can be imagined? Yes, it is, unless you know the rest of the story. Suffering can't be pushed to the side as a minor and unfortunate part of human life, and it can't be separated from God's own chosen experience or God's call on our lives. The apparent poor performance of Jesus in this world isn't seen for what it really was apart from becoming aware of *who God really is*. We must come to know how God really works in this world or we'll never really know God or who we are supposed to be as followers of Jesus.

Suffering lies at the heart of it all—who God is, how God works in an evil world, and who we are to be as God's faithful children. Even Jesus cried, hurt, and died. Our hearts are also to be broken. If deliberately pursuing pain is taking the matter too far, avoiding suffering to protect our own comfort and advantage is not taking it nearly far enough. Jesus felt deeply, accepted pain, cried with grief, and so must we. Why? Because suffering is God's heart and an essential aspect of life as God's faithful children.

Pain and God's Love

Suffering raises the most demanding questions for us humans. Simple answers aren't adequate in the face of suffering. The Bible's understanding of suffering is nuanced and multidimensional. For example, when weighing the biblical material, we see a critical balance. God is both a sovereign and a suffering God, all-powerful even when hanging on a cross. Really? Both? Yes! The truth is caught between these two truths.[54]

It's hard to accept the fact that even the best people suffer. The earliest Christians were told that they "had to suffer various trials." Why? It was so that the genuineness of their faith, once tested by fire, would result in praise, glory, and honor when Jesus would be revealed. They were not to be surprised even at "fiery ordeals" because they would be "sharing in Christ's sufferings" (1 Pet 4:13). Apparently, to be like God is to risk hurting like God.

Such teaching raises many questions. The fact is that being good doesn't necessarily lead to being safe or comfortable. That unfortunate fact applies to us, the best of us. If a preacher is saying that believing strongly enough in Jesus will definitely bring prosperity and guaranteed healing of whatever your disease or handicap, change the channel, go to another website, or try the church down the street that might read the Bible more closely.

Raise your own questions when a teacher in church says that God is so supreme that our rotten decisions cannot hurt God or change his mind. According to the Bible, we're dealing with a God who chooses *dialogue* and "partakes exactly of the qualities of complexity, dynamism, and fluidity that belong to the post-modern world."[55] That's actually good news. The all-powerful God is not remote from us and mechanical in relation to us. Why? Because God is love and ready, able, and anxious to make commitments to us, be impacted by our decisions, and weave a fresh pattern of redemption out of the very threads of our waywardness.

Neither Israel nor the church could escape the harsh realities of history. Christianity is not a religion of the timeless eternal separated from a timely history. God "is not out there beyond the starry sky, unaware of and untouched by the wailing of an abandoned child. God is in the very midst of suffering, not as its cause but as its victim!"[56] Jesus knew the worst of this gone-wrong world and yet "knew that the strong and steady undertone of life is joy . . . because all its dark mysteries are held in love."[57]

We humans, even those of us who believe in Jesus, must live in the real world and suffer something because of it. But why Jesus? Why would God himself have to join us and be subject to the worst of suffering at the hands of mere creatures? Of all people, why would Jesus, the Son of the Father, also be a man of sorrows, the one who must undergo great suffering?

> Suffering lies at the heart of who God is, how God works in an evil world, and who God's faithful children are supposed to be.

That seems wrong. The New Testament, however, makes two things clear. Jesus did suffer greatly and, even so, was not a victim of historical forces. He chose this lowly path and now calls on his followers to do the same.

Jesus "suffered under Pontius Pilate," says the Apostles' Creed. When Christians affirm this creed, they acknowledge the conflict between good and evil and pledge resistance to it—a chosen openness to suffering. How significant that the only human named in this classic creed is Pontius Pilate, the one who made the call to crucify the innocent Jesus. He did the wrong thing because he was afraid to do the right thing. Freeing Jesus would have caused riots and maybe cost Pilate his own job. So he made the fateful decision.

The bottom line? "The Empire through Pilate could make Jesus suffer . . . but it could not keep him from being the Son of God with power, the

Lord of all mankind, ruling from his unseen throne and destined one day to judge the world."[58]

The disciples of Jesus were typical Jews of that time. They hoped for liberation from Roman occupation of their land. They wanted a warrior king, a champion of their just cause, a Messiah who would put all things right. But the Gospels tell a different story. They focus on the "passion" of Jesus, an ugly jumble of his humiliation, betrayal, abandonment, and torture, leading to a brutal execution because he was an embarrassment to the religious establishment and a possible enemy of the state.

This dear Jesus, full of love and forgiveness, was distressingly open to suffering that his disciples were sure could have been avoided. They tried to warn and stop him. But he went right on and paid the worst of prices. Why? Because Jesus came from a different place, representing a sorrowing and self-sacrificing Father. Even more, he was that Father choosing to be with us in our misery. His words were about meekness and the arriving reign of divine love. Instead of waving a flag of power, Jesus wove the threads of love into the beginning of a new age.

Jesus is the ultimate example of a major point of the large Joseph story in the Old Testament. "You meant evil against me, *but God*..." Even though his brothers had sold him into slavery, Joseph used sewing imagery to tell them that "God, the Master Weaver, stretches the yarn and intertwines the colors, the ragged twine with the velvet strings, the pains with the pleasures.... He passes the shuttle back and forth across the generations, and as he does, a design emerges. Satan weaves; God reweaves."[59]

The loving Jesus would be dragged to a cross. The reweaving Father would refashion that cross into an instrument of salvation. From temporary pain would arise eternal joy. Given Jesus' understanding of his Father and his own mission, it's not surprising that he would open himself to suffering on our behalf. God's love acts like that. Voluntary vulnerability is a reflection of self-giving love, a Godlike love, a willingness to risk wounds to make forgiveness, new life, and true community possible. Death would be accepted in order that life might be liberated.

Some people picture God as a huge Judge sitting high above with an eagle eye and a huge gavel, always ready, maybe even anxious to slam it down on the cosmic podium when anything unacceptable is spotted. "Guilty!" "Play My Way Or Pay!" "No Deviance Will Be Tolerated!" "Rome Will Be Crushed!" "I Will Keep My People Safe from All Enemies!" But, according to Jesus, seeing the lowly man of sorrows from Nazareth is to see into the depths of the Father's heart (John 14:9).

Jesus looks across the valley to a wayward Jerusalem and tears flow down his cheeks (Luke 19:41). That means that there are tears watering the heart of God. Those eagle eyes of the Eternal One are actually glazed over with an infinite compassion for the guilty, lost, and suffering. Biblical revelation shows God as both ruling over creation and intimately and lovingly interacting with it. God is lovingly relational by nature. God is moved deeply by what happens here below.

Our deeds grieve and gladden, frustrate, and anger God. God's view of our waywardness is not lacking in judgment, but is covered in love. God's use of coercive power is disciplined by that love. The power is real and sometimes used, but God is slow to anger and reluctant to give up on and punish the wayward. Love leads, seeking redemption. As the prophet Hosea learned and demonstrated with his marriage to Gomer, God typically is patient, forgiving, working toward restoration. Grace is abundant; the use of coercive power is a sad last resort.

This truth shines everywhere through Scripture. God suffers *because of* his people. He seeks covenantal relationship and grieves when the relationship is broken by wayward partners. God suffers *with* his people, carrying the pain of sin and accepting its cost—that's where the cross of Jesus comes in. Explains a wise theologian: "The Father suffers the death of his Son and the Spirit feels both the Father's pain and the Son's self-surrender . . . . Paradoxically, when God's absence was most apparent on the cross, God's presence was most profoundly revealed."[60]

Check Genesis 32, where the strange story is told of Jacob wrestling all night with God. The weary man emerged with a broken hip and fresh identity and destiny. God allowed the match to happen and took something of a beating himself because Jacob needed the encounter so badly. Did you get that? God took a beating! The God who created the universe was open to sharing pain in order to redeem and bless. That's a different way of viewing "sovereignty." What a different God, the riverside wrestler, so high in being and yet, out of a loving heart, coming so low by choice to engage lost people. That's a God we can both worship in reverence and love in intimate relationship.[61]

When I was a college student, I was made to memorize Isaiah chapter 53 and write it from memory on the final exam. The professor said these verses were the highlight of the Old Testament, a picture of the coming

Messiah, the very heart and plan of God for us sinners. But its message seems backwards and unfair, nearly unbelievable. God is shown to be a Suffering Servant. No wonder Jesus cried.

God came to be with us as a man who would be despised by us humans and pierced for our wrongs, and without even opening his mouth to protest. Unbelievable! God comes to us for saving purposes and has a bad time of it. Jesus prayed in the garden, crying to his Father. If only the coming suffering could be avoided; but it couldn't be and he knew it.

Why not? Why couldn't suffering be avoided? The answer is amazing. It's because God would be on that cross personally! The reaching love of God was prepared to do no less on our behalf. Here lies the very nature of God and the center of the Christian faith and life: "When the crucified Jesus is called 'the image of the invisible God,' the meaning is that *this* is God, and God is like *this*. God is not greater than he is in this humiliation. God is not more glorious than he is in this self-surrender. God is not more powerful than he is in this helplessness. God is not more divine than he is in this humanity."[62]

> We know God best at the point of maximum pain—the crucifixion of Jesus. The tears of Jesus were the watery reflections of the reaching love of God.

The tears and pain of Jesus were the tears and pain of God. The cross of Jesus was located in the heart of God before it was planted in the hill outside Jerusalem. God is "the God who yearns parentally towards creation, the God who is not power*less* but whose power expresses itself unexpectedly in the weakness of love."[63]

Pushing God Off the Throne

It's not easy to agree with Hebrews 2:10. We're told that the pioneer of our salvation was made "perfect through sufferings." But why did Jesus need to be made perfect in the first place? Wasn't he always perfect? And more, why would his process of being perfected have to come through suffering? Many "evangelical" Christians resist the biblical answer. They want to protect God from being pulled off the divine throne, assuming that humans inflicting pain on God could reduce God to a deposed has-been.

Pushing God off the eternal throne can't happen, of course. The real issue is God's true identity as that throne is eternally occupied. The biblical answer is straightforward and quite amazing. *God is love*, which is why God suffers. Loving our fallen world is to suffer. God went so far as to yield his Son to suffering on our behalf. "Suffering is down at the center of things, deep down where the meaning is. Suffering is the meaning of our world. The tears of God are the meaning of history."[64] Yes, Jesus cried, and his tears were those of God.

It's a profound and basic truth. "God's problem is not that God is not *able* to do certain things. God's problem is that God loves! Love complicates the life of God as it complicates every life. God's *power* has ultimately to articulate itself in divine solidarity with the sufferer, that is, in the 'weakness' of suffering love."[65] Jesus could have avoided the cross, but only by becoming someone other than Jesus, Son of the Father.

The cross of Jesus speaks dramatically to the past and the future, spanning all human history. It somehow secured the defeat of evil from the past and guaranteed a final defeat of evil in the future. According to John, there will be a renewal of all things when every tear is wiped away. Never again will there be hunger or thirst. The sun will not beat down with scorching heat. The sacrificed Lamb will reign supreme and be the source of springs of living water. God will wipe away every tear from our eyes (Rev 7: 16–17).

Meanwhile, the crying of Jesus is a reflection in this world of the flowing tears of God in the eternities. "The omnipotent, in one instant, made himself breakable. He who had been spirit became pierceable. He who was larger than the universe became an embryo. And he who sustains the world with a word chose to be dependent upon the nourishment of a young girl."[66] This costly self-giving clarifies the nature of God and becomes the heart of Christianity.

We hear from the cross of Jesus these painful words: "My God, my God, why hast Thou forsaken me?" This cry of abandonment is "either the end of every theology and every religion or it is the beginning of a truly Christian theology."[67] The suffering of Jesus on our behalf is the action of a loving God. The truth was not abandonment but a launching of the hope of the ages. Suffering is the way Christ became like us and redeemed us, and also a main way that we can become like Jesus and minister through his Spirit to our broken world.

Objections keep coming. If God is all-everything—powerful, knowing, etc.—surely God can't be impacted negatively by us little human beings. The great healer surely can't be hurt. But the Bible says otherwise. God indeed is all-everything, including and especially all-love. That love reaches, risks, becomes vulnerable voluntarily, opens itself to the hurt of possible rejection.

That's the biblical story—God reaching, our failing, God in tears, God in pain for our salvation. It's about love risking and paying the price so that we might come home and again be whole. The story is not one of God falling off the divine throne; it's about God shining in glorious, loving splendor even from the cross!

The Source who stands above is also the Savior who stoops below. It's in the stooping that we understand most fully the standing. Here is the central point of our knowing God. "The distinctive place where the God of the biblical witness intersected the life process of creation was *at the point of pain*. Here emerges a distinctive view of God as simultaneously sovereign over creation and suffering with creation."[68]

When pain comes, we are instructed by Paul to gaze on the great pain of God. John Bunyan was correct. At the sight of the cross of Jesus, the burden fell off Christian's back and was never seen again. Suffering was not eliminated, but it had lost its backbreaking power. Because of the cross, wisdom broke into plain sight. Jesus cried as a result of the self-sacrificing love of a brokenhearted God. Realizing that should be the start of new life for us.

An arresting scene is that of Jesus looking across the valley and sorrowing over the history and future of his beloved Jerusalem. He who was there when all was created, he who would soon be sitting at the right hand of the Father, was sitting there crying! Added to that scene is the central symbol of the Christian faith, the cross, that awful place and horrendous means of the worst of all suffering, God's suffering.

God's way with this world is not always what we want when we hurt. We want instant results that relieve the pain and wipe out the injustice. But God's love is patient (1 Cor 13) and usually works to *empower* rather than *overpower*. This does not weaken God's power but shows its character. As John Wesley said, God works "strongly and sweetly." That is, God's grace works powerfully but not irresistibly.[69] Our dignity is not violated.

That old rugged cross would be the fate of Jesus, something that raises many questions for us humans. First, was it random fate or an actual choice as part of a plan? How did Jesus handle such pain? Why did he, of all people, have to endure such unjust suffering? How does a suffering Jesus represent the nature and work of the almighty God? How can the weakness of one man be the strength of all people, everywhere and always? Is there any way for us to be obedient children of God without following the suffering Jesus with our own suffering?

On go the tough questions. Does God suffer too? How can an all-powerful God be made to suffer by wayward creatures? Aren't "God" and "suffering" clashing words with opposite meanings? Is the cross a picture of God somehow at work for our salvation or the drama of powerful humans making a mockery of the humble and now failed Jesus? These are huge questions that deserve more than simplistic responses.

And what of the voices of the martyrs slain for their faithfulness to God? "How long, O Lord," they cry out, "how long will you wait to avenge your own"? (Rev. 6:9–10). Few things are so daunting to faith as the seeming slowness of God to act. Why won't or can't God respond to our prayers more visibly and immediately? Is our faith misplaced? Is it time to impeach the government of the universe as incompetent?

We hear God saying, "My thoughts are not your thoughts nor my ways your ways." "All right," we respond, "they're not, but can't you make your different thoughts plain so we can get through this turmoil of our hurting bodies and souls?" God seems to answer something like this: "Gaze at the cross of my Son, the depths of my suffering for the totality of your wrongdoing. Believe that, like my Son's experience, just ahead awaits a resurrection designed just for you!"

> God is not more powerful than he is in the helplessness of his incarnation in Jesus. God is not more divine than he is in this humanity.
>
> —Jürgen Moltmann

Standing Far Off

Mount Sinai is a huge hulk lurching upward from the desert floor. When covered by a black and threatening thundercloud, it becomes a mysterious place of ominous darkness, maybe hiding tornadoes, phantom furies, gigantic holes, and fiends of any and all kinds. Wisdom says to stay away. You'll surely get eaten up or swept away and lost forever in that swirling darkness.

The Bible tells us that the people of Israel did the smart thing. They "stood far off." But one man among them was bold indeed—maybe stupid. Moses "drew near to the thick darkness." He dared approach Mount Sinai when it was acting its worst. Not surprisingly, he was going it alone. Then comes this startling claim. In the midst of that awful darkness, among the hosts of frightening, rumbling, and unseen fiends, there was God! (Exod 20:21).

Our jagged journey of faith in this troubled world sometimes finds us in the dark places where it appears that God surely is not. A detour would be welcome, but none is available. The exile came and mocked the people of God, blanketing them with dark despair. The gas chambers later opened and swallowed Jews in mass. Atomic bombs fell and cities of humanity were reduced in seconds to a horror beyond description. An execution squad dragged the best of men to a hill called Golgotha and slaughtered him in public shame. And so it goes. Jesus warned that, while in him there is peace, in the world his disciples would have trouble—count on it (John 16:33).

A cancerous disease appears and eats away a helpless body, be the victim king or pauper, rich man or poor woman, lovely little child or world-class athlete. A distracted driver runs a light while texting and suddenly a whole family is ripped to pieces. A shattered romance or sudden business loss evaporates all savings. These are everyday events. They will find everyone in one way or another, leaving behind what appears to be only hopeless carnage. The sun goes down and darkness swallows everything. Even those of us who try to stand far off will succumb. The scourge comes after us and we cannot run forever.

But wait! The Bible tells another side of the story. Saul hated the Jesus people and was knocked from his horse outside the Damascus gate. He arose in darkness, blind, and emerged as Paul, a stalwart of the early church, a soul in hell brought to a heaven he had not dared believe existed. Peter betrayed his Lord and yet emerged an apostle. Best of all, Jesus himself, dead and sealed in a dark tomb, found his way into the dawn of a new day, the valley of the shadow of death transformed into the gate of a new creation. God was in the darkness and somehow it became light.

The mass of humanity trudges on in the darkness, despairing of any new day. We are lost, frightened, diseased, confused, abused, without apparent hope. We are of all skin colors, languages, religious traditions, and nationalities. Tragedy respects nothing. Suffering crosses all boundaries, enters every bedroom, rips relentlessly at all faiths. If those suffering should hear what Clement of Alexandria once said, they likely would think it shallow idealism. He said, "Christ turns all our sunsets into dawns." That sounds so good and can mean so little to someone still enveloped in a thick darkness.

On the other hand, what if it's true? What if the tears of Jesus are cleansing and healing? What if they are watery reflections of the reaching and saving love of God? What if God is in the midst of the darkness as the Light of the world, the Light only waiting for those far off to come near? What if Clement is right? Partnering with Christ, whatever the cost, can witness sunsets launching the night into a dawn heralding a new day.

To witness something that marvelous likely will involve some experienced unfairness and our resulting cry of innocence. We will have to read the book of Job carefully and rid ourselves of bad assumptions about the causes of suffering. We will have to deal with this: "When Christ calls a man, he bids him come and die."[70]

The God who come in the crying Jesus wants us to accept and reflect love, even when that choice involves pain. God wants our selfless deaths and faith commitments, not because we think they will feel good or likely will lead to desired rewards, but because of who God is and what we should and can become. We are called to cleave to God, as Job did, even when we seemingly have reasons to deny him. We are offered a gift that will make us new and transform us into agents of renewal for others.

GOD SAYS

My Grace is Sufficient!

(2 Cor 12:9)

7

SHOCK 'N AWE

But, God, I Didn't Do It! This Isn't Fair!

And those eighteen in Jerusalem the other day, the ones crushed and killed when the Tower of Siloam collapsed and fell on them, do you [Jesus] think they were worse citizens than all other Jerusalemites? Jesus responded. "Not at all." (Luke 13:1)

Once when the famous comedian Bob Hope received a major award, he responded, "I don't deserve this, but then I have arthritis and I don't deserve that either." Do we get only what we deserve in this life?

Evil is a heavy burden not easily explained in God's world. If Jesus really was God with us, the "very image of the invisible God" (Col 1:25), it's odd that he of all people had to cry. But evil is real and cry he did, and apparently so must we.

Is the presence of evil all our fault? If I'm hurting, does that mean that I've been sinning? Maybe, often, but maybe not. It's the classic drama of Job's situation. Explanations of the sources of evil are several and often not very helpful. Job's "friends" offered the usual perspectives before God called for all of them to be quiet.

Job, Shut Your Mouth!

It's an odd phrase, *shock 'n awe*, but it really fits what Job experienced. There was plenty of shock in his life and a desperate search for an answer to the apparent wrongness of all his suffering. How odd and seemingly unsatisfying is the great lesson that Job finally learned. It centered in an *awe* for God. We all tend to know the shock, but without basking in the awe.

We are being taught through Job's experience that regaining our awe, our reverence for the immensity that is God, is the only way to finally survive the shock of the injustices of this life. Why do good people suffer? The only adequate answer is glimpsing again the God who rises above all such questions. If God and God's ways were small enough to be fully understood by mere humans, God wouldn't be nearly big enough to deserve our worship.

Shock 'n awe didn't start as theological wisdom. It's a military phrase for rapid dominance. A spectacular display of force is supposed to overwhelm the enemy, paralyzing with the perception of the impossibility of surviving the onslaught. Overwhelmed, surrender is suddenly seen as the only available option. That's about how the confrontation played out for Job. His mouth closed only when the magnitude of God opened all around him and there was nowhere to hide.

Job was wise in resisting the cheap explanations of his friends. They kept saying that poor Job surely had sinned and was refusing to admit it, thus his suffering was the punishment of God. By Job 23 we see this suffering man turning away from such fruitless advice that was laced with religiously rigid and theologically shallow platitudes. He finally shifts inward in frustration and upward in bewilderment. Job was sure of at least one thing. If he got his day in the divine court, he would be vindicated by God. He knew that suffering is not always the direct result of the sin of the sufferer. He had not sinned and still he suffered. He cried out to God: "I didn't do it! This isn't fair!" He persisted in resisting his friends and questioning God.

Events were all wrong, unjustified, demanding an explanation that Job assumed only God could provide. But when the suffering man finally did get the divine answer recorded in Job 38, it wasn't what he'd hoped. It wasn't a logical explanation of why the awful suffering, a reasonable unraveling of what seemed so unjust. God answered more as a poet, thundering a blinding display of the divine glory. God showered down disabling questions that radiated from the unimaginable divine reality.

We sufferers want answers to questions that are without easy answers. There is mystery beyond our neat theories and scientific explanations. There is no one Bible verse that ends the mystery or one "friend" of Job who brings the definitive counsel. Says a wise man, "it is not *what* God says finally to the suffering Job but *that* God says something that is the answer. The Presence itself is the answer, and the only appropriate and convincing one, for all its elusiveness."[71]

God spoke by hurling impossible questions that stunned Job. They were: Who are you? Where were you? What do you know? Can you? God called on Job to stop looking for pat answers for suffering and instead stretch his imagination and consider the majestic panorama of creation. The poor man was taken on a whirlwind tour of the wonder of space, a tour that always reduces the smallness of mere humans to near nothing. Job's questioning of God had led to shock 'n awe, an awareness of how deep are the mysteries of God's ways that are embedded in the immensity of the creation and appear in the privacies of our personal suffering.

> We can survive the shocks of life without all the answers. The lesson Job learned centered in a great awe for God.

God's answer to Job's call for the "reasons" of his suffering were found less in detailed analysis and more in humbled awe, more as poetry and less as prose. The answers lie somewhere in the vistas of much larger things, somewhere in the vastness of the humanly incomprehensible, in the awesome arena of a loving and all-knowing God. Job finally realized that the best speaking he could do was falling silent.

This counsel remains crucial: "Blessed are we when we are poor in spirit and do not think we have our hands on the steering wheel of our own life. Let me be a feather on the breath of God."[72] To suffer often is to cry out with questions for which there are no easy answers. As G. K. Chesterton once put it, "The riddles of God are more satisfying than the solutions of man." There is meaning in the Creator's eyes, but it's beyond the little sphere of our seeing. The best seeing is to be lost in pure awe.

Bad Assumptions

The problem facing Job wasn't only the suffering itself and his lack of logical answers. It was his wrong working assumption. He assumed that the person who lives a good life in obedience to God will be rewarded with good fortune in this world—health, wealth, happiness. Those who choose to live otherwise will be punished accordingly. Surely this is the only just pattern of things under God. Surely, but apparently not.

The answer of God to Job puts a spotlight on Job's problem. It was not his suffering as much as his wrong assumption about its cause. This present world tends to function upside down. Goodness doesn't always bring quick reward and sin doesn't always bring immediate punishment. God's odd answer to Job from the distant skies can lead to two different impacts on our faith.

First, unrelenting and unexplained injustice can end our faith. If God doesn't clearly explain the suffering of good people and punish their enemies, maybe God isn't in control, is evil, or doesn't even exist. Second, suffering undeserved wrong can deepen our faith by enlarging our vision of what it means to be human in an evil world and how amazingly loving God is *despite everything*. The deepening option isn't automatic or easy as we travel the jagged journey of faith.

When William Sloane Coffin was a student at Yale, three of his friends were killed in a car accident. The driver had fallen asleep at the wheel. Coffin was sickened and angered at the funeral when the presiding priest announced, "The Lord gave and now has taken away." He actually considered tripping the priest when he marched up the aisle at the end of the service.[73] Surely that's not what had happened, God just deciding to have Coffin's friends dead!

My mouth almost dropped open when once I was standing with a family at a casket and heard the minister comfort the wife of the deceased by announcing, "God needed another tenor in the heavenly choir." Better to stand in silence than say something stupid, well-meaning or not. A close friend from high school died and this appeared in his little funeral folder: "God broke our hearts to prove to us He only takes the best." Really? The deceased was special, granted, but is that how God acts? I hope not. I think not. But, then, what do I know?

What mere human, clergy or not, can penetrate the mysteries of good and evil, chance and fate, justice and injustice, the ways of God? According to Job (and the rest of the Bible), we can know at least this. God is there, hears our cries of pain, cares deeply about us, and is ready to speak to us in our confusion and misery. The divine voice may not answer our questions as we choose to pose them, but the very presence of a divine voice should be enough to satisfy. The enough is verbalized well in verse one of the famous Irish hymn "Be Thou My Vision": "Not be all else to me, save that Thou art."

Let's be clear about the bad assumptions we often make when facing evil in any form. Few things are as dangerous as a one-sided truth. In fact, most heresies in the history of Christian theology have not been complete falsehoods but pieces of a truth parading as the whole. For example, was Jesus truly God or truly human? The only adequate answer is "Yes!" To avoid a bad assumption rooted in only half of a truth, it's not one or the other but the awkwardness of both.[74]

> Is my suffering my fault or God's? There are four common assumptions, each slightly right and, by itself, dangerously wrong.

Look carefully at the easy answers parading around as simplistic solutions to complex questions. They're probably more wrong than right. Regarding suffering, here are four common assumptions that are slightly right and, by themselves, dangerously wrong.

1. **All Suffering Comes from God.** Since God is God, surely all that happens is caused and controlled by God. There is a detailed divine plan for each of our lives. Our paths and destinies are predetermined. God is sovereign. All must accommodate to God's will. "African slaves were told by Christian pastors that their plight was the will of God. Battered women are sent back to their violent husbands. Public religious voices preached the destruction of 9/11 as retribution for the behaviors of feminists, abolitionists, pagans, gays and lesbians."[75]

    That's true, sort of, to a point, maybe. But the fuller truth is that God, whose very heart is love, has created this world in such a way that sin, suffering, and injustice are real possibilities. That hardly means that God is the immediate cause of all that happens. That would be a rigid determinism or mechanical predestinationism that dispenses with human freedom (part of God's good creation). Much suffering comes not from God's advance choices but from the misuse of our freedom. God intends no sin or suffering.

    Philip Yancey reports in his *Where Is God When It Hurts?* that he once watched a television interview with a famous Hollywood actress. Her lover had drowned near Los Angeles because he had rolled off a yacht in a drunken stupor. The grieving actress looked at the camera and asked, "How could a loving God let this happen?" Was that the right question? Wasn't it the man's behavior that caused the tragedy?

2. **All Suffering Is Caused by the Sin of the Sufferer.** If a person honors the moral order of this world, life will go well. Suffering is a wake-up call that repentance is required. If you're suffering now, it's likely the deserved result of what you did earlier in life, or even in former lives. If you improve your current performance, your future life or lives will be better. Your soul is released into divine bliss only when all your sins have been admitted and paid for. Karma? Purgatory?

   Such teaching is common in Christian circles in one form or another. It's true, sort of, to a point, maybe. The fuller truth is that, although suffering often is our own fault, or the fault of other sinful humans, it certainly isn't always. The Jews were told as they entered the promised land to worship and obey God and they would be assured life and blessing; fail to do so and evil and death would result (Deut 30). That was direct cause-and-effect thinking, quite understandable, not necessarily correct.

   Job's "friends" assumed wrongly that the suffering that was raining down on Job was from his sin and should be confessed. The disciples of Jesus met a man blind from birth and asked whether he or his parents had sinned to bring this on him. Responded Jesus, neither the man nor his parents (John 9:1). They were posing the wrong question, making the wrong assumption.

   "The root of suffering is attachment"
   The Buddha

3. **All Suffering Is Illusion.** We must transcend ourselves. Buddhism teaches that suffering comes not from God or our past deeds but from our own excessive desires. The solution to suffering is a change of consciousness, the extinguishing of our desires, detaching ourselves from transitory things and persons. We must get over the intense individuality of today's Western societies that elevates our personal rights and hunger for more things, greater beauty, longer life. Wanting leads to frustration and suffering. Wanting nothing is to have everything.

   That's true, sort of, to a point, maybe. It's true that many of our human anxieties and even physical ills have their origins in our minds and frustrated desires. Psychotherapists work to unpack the past that has perverted our present. Not desiring more is already to have enough. Even so, many maladies are objectively real and do not originate with God, our own past actions, or our own fears, conditioning, and excessive desires. Denying the actual reality of a suffering situation is hardly helpful. Much suffering is more than illusion.

4. **All Suffering Is Random.** Here's a classic statement of the secular view so common today. "In a universe of blind physical forces and genetic replication, some people are going to get hurt, other people are going to get lucky, and you won't find any rhyme or reason in it, nor any justice. The universe that we observe has precisely the properties we should expect if there is, at bottom, no design, no purpose, no evil, no good, nothing but pitiless indifference."[76] Suffering will happen randomly. No one is to blame. It's just how it is.

From a Christian viewpoint, this approach is slightly true and fundamentally wrong. There are random injustices that have no apparent reason to them. People get caught in natural disasters, for instance. They just happened to be in the wrong place at the wrong time. But our faith says that God is. There is purpose in the flow of our history. There is a difference between good and evil that's built into the very fabric of creation. The Ten Commandments are not arbitrary ethical guidelines but fundamental principles of how life works properly. All suffering is not merely random even if explanations for it elude us.

We say "No!" to these four bad assumptions. At best, they are half-truths. We agree with this bottom line: "We have examined some fractional answers to the problem of pain and found them thin rations. Pain is not unreal . . . not a legacy from prior incarnations . . . doesn't all come from sin . . . . There are no prefabricated answers, but there is an Answer."[77] It's that overarching Answer for which we are hunting. Maybe the answer is the *Presence of the Answerer*. God transcends our feeble questions, but comes in love, cries over our sin, stands with us, and points to a new age soon to come.

Suffering is very real and can't quickly, rightly, and always be blamed on God, something we did, just the phantoms conjured up by our fanciful imaginations and frustrated desires, or the world of "no design, no purpose, no evil, no good, nothing but pitiless indifference." Such thinking is very unbiblical, non-Christian.

Timothy Keller offers wisdom that mirrors the view of Jesus. "Christianity teaches that, contra fatalism, suffering is overwhelming; contra

Buddhism, suffering is real; contra karma, suffering is often unfair; but contra secularism, suffering is meaningful. There is a purpose to it, and if faced rightly, it can drive us like a nail deep into the love of God and into more stability and spiritual power than you can imagine."[78]

Is the core of our human existence negative or positive? The ancients tended to opt for the negative. Make merry in the moment as you can, then fate takes over and tomorrow becomes full of nothing. At least you will have had the merriment of today. Followers of Jesus, reflecting the biblical tradition, thought more positively: "While other worldviews lead us to sit in the midst of life's joys, foreseeing the coming sorrows, Christianity empowers its people to sit in the midst of this world's sorrows, *tasting the coming joy*."[79]

This reversal of perspective is so significant. This is why there is a tradition of Christians being able to suffer better than others. They can see purpose in the present and hope for the future, even if they don't have answers to all the questions that suffering brings. What they do have is the gift of the Spirit's presence as an advance taste and pledge of an assured future inheritance (Rom 8:23; 2 Cor 1:22, 5:5; Eph 1:14).

God finally answered Job. When he could get himself back together, Job responded back to God (chap. 42). He had not been beaten into submission by a bigger foe so much as honored by God's presence and humbled by God's greatness. He still didn't have full answers to his urgent questions, a detailed theology of suffering, a comprehensive map of the origins and meanings of his problems, but he did have something that was enough.

> God stands far above our limited thoughts. What comforts us is *the Presence*, as was known by the three young Jewish men in an awful Babylonian furnace.

Job had the honor of knowing God and the dignity of knowing himself better and realizing that he could go on with life without having all the answers. He now knew that there is no quick cause-and-effect equation that explains all events, no human way of calculating for sure the immediate sources and results of good and bad actions. He had become comfortable with not knowing what can't be known. That's spiritual maturity. It's the ability to rise above circumstance.

No theory of the reason for suffering fits all cases. God can't always be quoted as our last word on why sickness and injustice and death come. God stands far above our limited thoughts and meager speech. What we do have to comfort us is *the Presence* as was once known by three young men in an awful Babylonian furnace.

Nebuchadnezzar was sure that he had thrown into the furnace only three men, but clearly there now was a fourth like the Son of God (Dan 3). The faithful had not been spared an unjust punishment or given all answers as to why it had to be, but they had been graced with a companion who would sustain them through it all—and even find ways to bring good out a bad circumstance.

Will we always understand? No. Will we ever be abandoned. NO! Although we walk into the very shadow of death, God will be there with us (Ps 23). Said Jesus, as reported at the very end of Matthew's gospel, "And remember, I am with you always, to the end of the age." When we are shocked by negative circumstances we should stand in quiet awe and reverence of the one who stands above all circumstances and loves us in amazing and eternal ways. Suffering can bring doubts; spiritual maturity brings a readiness to doubt even our doubts.

DOUBT YOUR DOUBTS

Any Chance that Our Doubts Themselves Deserve Doubting?

Live your questions now, and perhaps even without knowing it, you will live along some distant day into your answers.

—Rainer Maria Rilke

When we look for a deliverer who will crush the opposition by superior force, we find instead a servant-messiah who allows himself to the crushed and bruised for us. What kind of God is this?

—Philip Kenneson, Life on the Vine

In the intellectual life of any thoughtful Christian, doubt can't be avoided. Nor should it be a cause of guilt. We humans have to live by faith and the faith journey is a jagged one. It jockeys between believing and not being so sure. After all, evil is very real and faith might be self-delusion, or it can be the key to opening a larger reality beyond the suffering and confusion of the present time.

Rainer Maria Rilke is a poet with wisdom to share. When frustration, uncertainty, and pain trouble us, what should we do? Quit? Question? Doubt? No, we should *move on*, taking the questions with us. We should look for the day when time, experience, and persistent faith somehow have moved us beyond the questions into the arena of satisfactory solutions—or at least a comfort with not knowing beyond doubt.

Albert Schweitzer once said, "I don't know what your destiny will be, but one thing I know: the only ones among you who will be really happy are those who will have sought and found how to serve." In other words, when it hurts and solutions aren't in sight, when hope is fading and the goal seems far away, when you're wondering about your faith, give yourself away to others. That way, somehow, sometime, things will get resolved for the best.

I'll say it again. For the thoughtful believer in this kind of world, doubts are inevitable, especially when suffering comes. But don't stop there. Doubting your doubts should also happen. It's part of a maturing wisdom. Ask God whatever you will. Be warned, however. "If you want to manipulate God for your own agenda, forget it. God is God! But if you're crying out in repentance and love, seeking the highest good of others and wanting to be made more like Christ and better able to serve, then God says to you, 'Bring on your questions!'"[80]

Don't Just Lie There!

Pain, doubt, unanswered questions. What should be done? What can be done? Poet Rilke says to move on. Schweitzer advises looking beyond oneself to see if someone else needs help you could give. The New Testament offers similar advice, coming directly from the mouth of Jesus. The story goes like this in Luke 17.

There were ten lepers approaching Jesus and begging for healing. "Keeping their distance, they called out, saying, 'Jesus, Master, have mercy on us!' When he saw them, he said to them, 'Go and show yourselves to the priests.' And, *as they went*, they were made clean." Did you get that

> For a thoughtful believer, doubts are inevitable, especially when suffering comes. But doubts also should be doubted.

timing? They were to go to the priests for authentication of their healing but would have to start out with the ugly disease still all over them! They were to go in faith that once they got to the priests they would get a great report. Somewhere *during the trip* to the priests there would be the miraculous event. For it to happen, however, they had to believe while still diseased. They had to get up and go on faith in Jesus' words and promise.

When your world goes wrong, don't just lie there feeling sorry for yourself. Get up and plunge into the jagged journey, believing that God waits somewhere along the way with healing in his wings. Suffering can initiate the hurting soul into depths of insight and joy that the outside onlooker can never know. Recall these lines of wisdom from Robert Browning Hamilton:

> I walked a mile with Pleasure,
> She chattered all the way,
> But left me none the wiser
> For all she had to say.
>
> I walked a mile with Sorrow,
> And ne'er a word said she;
> But, oh, the things I learned from her,
> When Sorrow walked with me!

Also note these ancient lines:

> Let this darkness be a bell tower and you the bell.
> As you ring, what batters you becomes your strength.
> Move back and forth into the change.
> What is it like, such intensity of pain?
> If the drink is bitter, turn yourself to wine.[81]

There's a needed caution to these words. It involves something other than our gaining strength just by the "turn yourself" in the last line. Required of the Christian is more than sheer willpower. The necessary turning must be enabled by the unmerited and yet available grace of a loving God.

The cross of Jesus is a dramatic symbol of suffering that screams of pain and injustice. Why, then, does such an ugly and unwelcome thing continue to haunt the imagination and conscience of humanity? Why the classic lines, "In the cross of Christ I glory, Towering o'er the wrecks of time?" It's because that cross is sorrow walking with us, talking to us, teaching us what we most need to know. On that cross, eternity intersected time and God spoke. In this pain of God is the healing of humanity!

How odd to think that looking at that awful crucifixion scene outside Jerusalem could ever be reason to get up and dance! But Henri Nouwen says that "mourning and dancing are part of the same movement of grace."[82] We must learn to face painful loss head on and deliberately connect our suffering with that of the world around us. Pursuing the holy life involves our choice to exercise compassion. Such exercise initiates us into the larger community of suffering. The burden becomes mutual, and lighter. Others must be allowed to help us carry our pain while we are reaching out to carry theirs. In the reaching and the carrying comes a holy healing.

> Realizing the helpful possibilities of honest doubt frees a believer to plunge more deeply into an honest faith.

God reached, suffered, carried the weight of the sin of the whole world. In that crisis of the cross lies our eternal healing. Sharing this amazing news with others can be their healing. Don't doubt this until you've really tried it. If you try, allowing God's healing arms to envelop you, your doubts in time will dissipate into dance.

The holy lives of Jesus' followers will be wonder-full if not pain free. Christians will suffer in this world, but the suffering will be a sharing in the sufferings of Jesus, maybe even an experiencing of the baptism of blood that will usher persecuted believers into the heavenly feast of the coming better world (1 Pet 4:12–5:11). No matter. It's participation in God's life and work and future.

When trouble comes, when our private and even public worlds convulse, what should we do? It's natural to run and hide if we can find somewhere safe. In the Great Depression of the 1930s, the wonderful musicals of the team of Fred Astaire and Ginger Rogers helped America dance its way through deep trouble—*Top Hat* in 1935, *Swing Time* in 1936, *Shall We Dance* in 1937, etc. It may have been escapist entertainment, but it was timely and most welcome. Is that enough for Christians?

How should we act while waiting on the action that only God can take? Paul was worrying about this question early in the church's life. He told the Roman Christians that there was no safe place to hide. Instead of hiding, they should keep an eye on the clock, get out of bed, and get dressed! "Wake up from your slumber . . . . The night is nearly over . . . . Clothe yourselves with the Lord Jesus Christ . . ." (Rom 13:11–14). We dare not be naked in this suffering world. We must be fully dressed and active as advance agents of God's coming again.

Jesus left us his Spirit as a foretaste of God's coming future. We now are to be sharing this great menu, this tasty bite today of God's coming tomorrow, helping others sample its goodness. We are to be light-spreaders in the darkness before God's coming dawn. Paul told the Thessalonians, and now us, "May the Master pour on the love so that it fills your lives and splashes over on everyone around you" (1 Thess 3:12). Said Dietrich Bonhoeffer, "Your life as a Christian should make non-believers question their disbelief in God." As they see you dancing, even in your suffering, they're forced to think again.

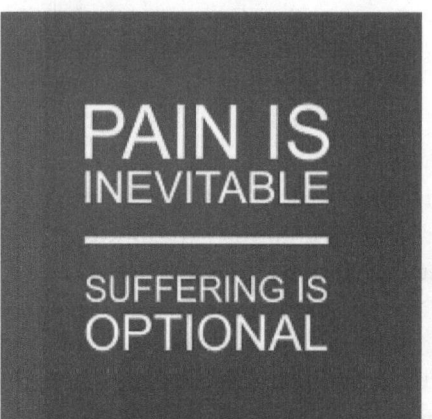

That's what it means to be an advance agent of God's coming again. It's time to get up and dressed in the full armor of the Spirit. God's tomorrow is about to dawn! The baby in the Bethlehem feeding trough now is sitting at God's right hand. So . . . get out of bed, get dressed in Christ, put on the full armor of the Spirit, and be about the Master's work before he comes again. Do it in the midst of today's suffering, sometimes in spite of it, sometimes even through it, even with its assistance. Be faithful, head for the priests as instructed (Luke 17), and your healing may come in route.

Permission to Doubt

The word *doubt* has gotten bad press in the vocabulary of Christian living. Faith is the victory that overcomes the world, so we say and sing, while doubt is faith's chief enemy. Still, all of us who believe experience our times of doubt, unless we live in a state of denial or a thoughtless void. Hope can fail when hurt increases. Faith can falter when suffering surges. We all have a stake in that ancient prayer, "Lord, I believe; help my unbelief" (Mark 9:24).

A real advance in the life of faith awaits believers in God when they finally develop a more realistic and wholesome attitude toward the doubt they occasionally experience and tend to repress, even try hiding from the all-seeing God. We must move beyond feeling guilty for doubting our faith and questioning God. Indeed, there may be more genuine faith in honest doubt than in the blind believing of some conventional creed.

Helmut Thielicke was once thinking about the devastated Germany after the mass bombings of World War II. He was trying to balance visions of great suffering, rampant evil, real faith, and encroaching doubt. He said: "He who knows what faith is must also have stood beneath the baleful eye of that demonic power against which we fling our faith. Faith is either a struggle or it is nothing."[83]

There is a certain degree of uncertainty in faith that cannot be removed—else faith is no longer faith but unquestionable fact. There is a certain "leap" in faith that exercises the courage to embrace that which cannot be fully comprehended. It is to trust that which is never totally beyond the reach of honest doubt. Faith that faces suffering head on must always leave room for mystery and risk despair.

If there is never any doubt, it's questionable if there is ever any genuine faith. The mature person has little fear of being self-critical. The hurting person should feel no shame from a little questioning of the things of God. Only the immature fancy their own reasoning above question. Honest doubts are one means of the ongoing refinement of faith. They are evidence of appropriate humility. They tend to expose false securities and undermine idolatrous views.

Realizing the helpful possibilities of honest doubt frees a believer to plunge more deeply into an honest faith. Job's "friends" pounded him with accusations. "Job, poor guy, you must have done something very wrong or you wouldn't be hurting like this. Just confess it and get yourself forgiven and healed." But Job knew better and stood his ground while still having no answers. He looked upward for help. Such direct questioning of God was at home in the Jewish tradition. It shows "a sublime confidence that to ask ultimate questions of God is not to turn away from him but to draw nearer to him."[84]

Some think that Job 9:22–24 shouldn't have made it into in the Bible. Job boldly calls into question the basic beliefs of the Jews. Even so, the defiant speech made the sacred text because the Jews believed two things. First, the darkness should not be denied nor is it the case that darkness is necessarily all of reality. Even when things are at their worst, even when God seems wholly absent, God is still the One with whom we must deal.

Second was the conviction of Israel that people in the pit of life's pain and injustice may still turn to this sovereign One and find him "passionately attentive."[85] We still may not fully understand or hear what we want.

Even so, we will realize that God is always there, always cares deeply, and will have the last word—evil never will.

There should come a point when the thoughtful believer increasingly doubts his or her own doubts and comes to champion the great word of faith. That word is "nevertheless!" Of course, the facts of life have a way of disrupting our little theories of how things ought to be. Our generalizations get contradicted, our dogmas dynamited. Still, the disruptions don't deserve the last word. Beyond the unanswered questions comes the persistent faith assertion, nevertheless!

Sometimes the only available answer to persisting evil and unanswered questions is to choose to trust anyway. The hymn "Trust and Obey" is as profound as simple. Why trust and obey? "For there's no other way to be happy in Jesus, but to trust and obey."

A journey taken by many Christians runs from "acquiescent acceptance" to experiencing the disillusionment coming from life's battering of faith's idealisms. Finally, however, many also become ashamed of being ashamed of the gospel of Christ. Here's the proper path, a bit jagged but always headed in the right direction. Look again at the *8-9-10* or *O-D-R* paths introduced earlier. Faith's orientation faces disorientation and then can (should) rise to an ever higher reorientation.

We believe routinely, then encounter hard questions and harsh alternatives. Finally, we realize the considerable downsides of the critics of our faith. We come to doubt our doubts, become disillusioned about our disillusionments, and choose to reclaim our faith, chastened to be sure, but now more sturdy and mature.[86]

I've seen it so often with new students in a Christian university. The big world of learning and separation from home shake their simple Sunday school faith. Then, with time, thoughtfulness, and patient faculty, even their doubts get shaken. They finally come to be a senior with a belief that's deeper than before the freshman crisis. Passing through crisis can be disabling or wonderfully maturing.

Here's part of a sermon I preached to my home church in Anderson, Indiana, in 2006. I was recently remarried to Jan after the death of my first wife. "Why did Arlene die of cancer, an innocent woman so careful about her lifestyle? I don't know! Why did Jan's husband die of a sudden heart attack while at the wheel on an interstate? She doesn't know either. But, by faith, here's what *we do know*. God is holy, sovereign, and can be trusted with the future! (Ps 22:3–5). We sometimes lack answers, but need not lack hope. Jan and I doubted even our doubts and now were fortified by faith."

Welcoming the Stranger

Christian monks have been taught for centuries to welcome strangers. They have been told to think of them as Christ in their midst. Outsiders should not be shunned or, as some evangelicals seem to think, treated mostly as targets for evangelizing. "If we could capture them and change them into one of us, looking and thinking like us, then we would welcome them. Otherwise, they should stay outside. They have nothing to offer us except the arrival of new questions for which we haven't answers and new demands that we don't want to assume." That's an overdrawn stereotype, of course, but a real danger nonetheless.

Encountering strangers is always fraught with both promise and peril, a fresh treat or threat. Welcoming strangers is urgent in the multicultural world of today with its geography reduced to hours to anywhere and communication with almost anyone available instantly. And the biblical mandate is clear enough. Jesus had nowhere to lay his head (Matt 8:20), depended on the hospitality of others (Luke 10:38–42), and was buried in someone else's tomb (Matt 27:57–61). Therefore, "you shall also love the stranger, *for you were strangers* . . ." (Deut 10:19). Hospitality to strangers may lead to "entertaining angels without knowing it" (Heb 13:2) and even encountering the Divine in disguise (Matt 25:35).

> In any black night, look for a fresh possibility. The leaves of new life already may be fluttering high in the trees. Can you see and hear them?

Who are the uninvited outsiders at our doors? They are strangers precisely because they are different from us, unknown, possibly danger-bringing, doubt-raising, growth-demanding, sources of unnecessary suffering. Should we risk letting them in? We doubt it, and yet Christ calls us to get beyond our doubt, to see the stranger as a potential resource instead of a threat. Answer the door. Who knows who or what is arriving unexpectedly? It might be Jesus in unfamiliar clothes.

Jesus said, "Listen, Nicodemus, listen to the wind!" (John 3:8). He went on to explain to this intellectual religious leader something like this. "You have questions and want answers that satisfy your intellect and limited assumptions. But might there be realities beyond the reach of your mind?

Remember that the Spirit of God is the divine power who rustled over the original creation. That same Spirit has swept across the centuries as the constant possibility of new creation and fresh thoughts and insights. Dare to raise your sails to catch the wind. Don't fear where it might take you."

When something in life goes wrong, we are tempted to give in to cynicism, deciding that God sits in heaven and can be counted on to do nothing. Life is reduced to crude practicalities of the immediate moment. Faith is seduced to ground zero. Seeing a glass half full is being an optimist, half empty a pessimist. But if one is cynical of all faith options, he or she might see this as the real problem. The glass is twice as big as it should be!

The struggle with relentless cancer or a hateful family member tempts us to think that God's Spirit has fallen asleep, that the breath of God apparently has stopped warming this earth. The sails of life's ship sag badly for lack of energy and death lurks on the listless sea. But the encouraging voice of Jesus speaks to us, as to Nicodemus. "Listen! The wind may be slow-moving but it's nonetheless unmistakable. God stirs, moves, comes, is still brooding over the chaos, is sending the breath of new life. If only you will turn your faces into the path of God's birthing power."

In any black night, the Master says: "Open your window and listen carefully. Look and believe in a fresh possibility. The leaves of new life already may be fluttering high in the trees. Can't you see and hear them? No matter. Believe that God's dawn is close by and unstoppable. Do you doubt that, blinded by some suffering? Dare to doubt your doubt!"

9
NIGHT STARS

The Darker the Night the Brighter the Stars

God, brilliant Lord. . . I look up at your macro-skies, dark and enormous, your handmade sky-jewelry (Ps 8:1, 3).

In Isaiah 9:2 and Matthew 4:16 we're told that in the birth of Jesus "the people walking in darkness have seen a great light; on those living in the land of the shadow of death a light has dawned."

We saw in chapters seven and eight that just being human means getting rained and even hailed on sooner or later, Christian or not. This raises hard questions, but at some point we need to rise above them and dare to doubt even our doubts. The wisdom of life requires something other than the annulment of incongruity. It requires the achievement of a serenity that can exist within it. Night there will be. Stars in the night sky there are. In fact, the darker the night the brighter the stars shine.

To be responsible Christians, we must go to places where we know it will hurt, where there will be darkness. The love in God's heart led to voluntary suffering with and for us fallen humans. God's love now should be in us, leading us to engage and suffer with and for the world. Facing suffering with selfless courage will cast a painful shadow over us. Even so, the light can shine brightly regardless of the night. In fact, it may be that serving "the least of these" brings out the brightest night stars.

John launches his Gospel with this about the coming of Jesus: "The Life-Light blazed out of the darkness; the darkness couldn't put it out" (1:5). We who follow Jesus are likewise to shine into today's darkness as the light of love that the world cannot finally put out!

Deep Suffering and Intense Joy

In the midst of any hurt, there's always the option of looking up at the brilliant "sky-jewelry" that shines above. Should there be clouds when you look up, remember this. They are momentary distractions not affecting the reality of the blazing lights higher up. It's very possible to see a great light even when walking in darkness. It's possible to sing while suffering.

> It's very possible to see a great light even when walking in darkness and then sing while suffering.

Suffering is the great leveler that can undercut the illusion that we control the course of our lives. It tends to eat away our big egos. Suffering has the capacity for great good, a crucial enlightenment. For us, as for Jesus, it can be received as an invitation to surrender our lives to God, to open the heavy drapes to the morning light just outside. It tends to clear away clouds and reveal the stars that were there all the time.

There are two words that sound the same when spoken but mean very different things. They are "mourning" and "morning." Can they ever go together? Yes. Be compassionate, carry the burdens of others, mourn with those who mourn and a new morning will arrive. Said Jesus: "You're blessed when you care. At the moment of being 'care-full,' you find yourselves cared for" (Matt 5:7). The best often emerges from what appears to be the worst. A new morning emerges from a night of mourning. Note these wonderful words from an unknown hand:

> Out of the black and murky clouds,
> Descends the stainless snow.
> Out of the crawling earth-bound worm
> A butterfly is born.
> Out of the somber shrouded night,
> Behold! A golden morn!
> Out of the pain and stress of life,
> The peace of God pours down.

NIGHT STARS

> Out of the nails—the spear—the cross,
> Redemption—and a crown!

Yes, even the darkest night has its stars. In fact, the darker the brighter. Here's an insightful witness to an enlightening fact: "I look back on experiences that at the time seemed especially desolating and painful with particular satisfaction. Indeed, I can say with complete truthfulness that everything I have learned in my 75 years in this world, everything that has truly enhanced and enlightened my experience, has been through affliction and not through happiness."[87] Dark nights, bright stars.

A dramatic experience came one night when I was on the isolated plains of Zambia in central Africa. Ten of us were crossing the countryside packed in a van. We were on a mission of mercy and had to get to Lusaka by morning to conduct a pastor's conference. The driver stopped in the middle of nowhere for a necessary bathroom break. There were no facilities, of course, not a hint of human existence, no electricity for many miles in any direction.

Here's all he said. "Just walk behind the van until you are totally in the dark and then you can do your business. Be sure to stay on the hard surface of the road, however, since lions and snakes don't like it there so much. I'll count heads to be sure we all get back before I leave. I promise!"

I did disappear into the darkness, happily but cautiously, and survived whatever was there that I never saw. But I experienced much more than the relief I needed. The canopy above was ablaze with stars. Each seemed huge and heavy, sagging in the sky and drifting almost to earth. Some were so low on the horizon that it seemed they were threatening to touch the ground only a mile or two away. I'll never forget that amazing sight, one paid for by my being away from the distracting comforts of "civilization," vulnerably close to the glory and danger of nature in the raw. God's sky-jewelry was on grand display. Intense darkness made possible my seeing the bright lights.

The people who see are the ones who are in the right place and actually looking up regardless of potential danger and isolation. Here is the remarkable witness of a humbled Christian leader who had encountered a blind beggar on a third-world city street. Oddly, despite the man's seemingly desperate condition, he was singing. The music in his soul was coming from somewhere beyond the obvious circumstances.

Somehow "this eyeless pauper had discovered a candle called satisfaction and it glowed in his dark world. . . . Though the man I now saw was still sightless, he was remarkably insightful. And though I was the one with eyes, it was he who gave me a new vision."[88] Sight in the darkness; music in the city's clamor; joy in the soul when there is only loss on the surface. A twinkling star in the night is God's winking at one who is observant.

Paul could see joy in suffering (Rom 5:2–5), but his joy didn't come from just any suffering. His pain came from selfless obedience to Christ. "A gospel which has at its core the cross of the Christ must produce a fellowship whose life is marked by suffering."[89] The church can rejoice only when it's participating in the sacrificial suffering of Jesus. That's the suffering that unites the church with the suffering God and the suffering world that God loves so much. Suffer with God for the world and rejoice. Your mourning will be tinged by a bright new morning.

Richard Rohr speaks of a matured faith in which suffering and joy, light and dark combine naturally, even comfortably. "Our mature years are characterized by a kind of bright sadness and sober happiness, if that makes any sense.... There is still darkness in the second half of life—in fact maybe even more. But there is now a changed capacity to hold it creatively and with less anxiety. It is what John of the Cross called 'luminous darkness,' a coexistence of deep suffering and intense joy in the saints."[90]

When young, we have lots of questions about life and little patience with answers that don't immediately satisfy. Then time stretches out and eventually either hardens or seasons us, makes us cynical or more relaxed and accepting of questions not readily answered. The jagged journey of Christian faith can bruise or heal, discourage or strengthen. It tends either to deepen the relationship with God or sour it. It's our choice.

The challenge is clear. Stay connected, no matter what, stay in relationship with God. The darkness of where we are can be the stage for realizing how bright are the stars that shine above that very place. There indeed is a "luminous darkness" where suffering and joy can walk side by side. To be "in Christ" is to be in light's range despite any darkening circumstance.

The Old Testament tells the story of the jagged journey of the Jews—so much suffering threatening to darken their hope. The final editors of this story had their obvious agendas. One obviously was to keep hope alive in every darkness. The three large sections of the Old Testament all end on the same note and with the same intention, that of keeping hope alive in the night. In each case, the final word is—hold on, believe, reform, return, God is not done with you yet! Stay connected, stay true, look up and live.[91]

No Disconnecting from Pain

My wife retired after decades of high school teaching. She had been in touch constantly with the pain of her students, many coming from disadvantaged homes and acting out at school their lives' frustrations. Now retired, it could have been an easy chair for her, finally some isolation from the pain of others. That was an option, but not her choice, not what Jesus would have done or have her do. She got involved in the big food pantry ministry of our local church, really involved. Each week she touches lovingly a parade of pain, determined to do what she can, one hungry person at a time. The pantry is a dark place filled with many shafts of light—my wife being one of them.

Even if available, disconnecting is always the wrong option for a follower of Jesus. The faith is about connecting, being in right relationship with Jesus, his other disciples, and the hurting world to which Jesus is so lovingly connected. "Be with me," he was always saying to his disciples, "and with the poor and hurting to whom I and now you are called." Get connected. Touch the night. See the stars.

> Through every event, however untoward, there is always a way through to God. The way is selfless service to others. It may not be pain free, but it can be pleasure laden.

We are told that Jesus and certain of his disciples once were together on a mountaintop experiencing the dramatic revelation of Jesus as God in their midst. It was so wonderful an experience, such a spiritual high, that the disciples didn't want to leave and return to the grit and grime of the world below. But Jesus refused to let them keep basking in the glorious vision, relaxing in a tranquility that the mass of humans didn't know. He pointed them straight back to earth with its struggles and perplexities, exactly where they likely would be misunderstood and even persecuted.

The jagged path of faithful discipleship runs from transfiguration to costly self-giving. The disciples would have to go downward from the mountain, but now with an upwardness vibrating in their souls. They could go right into the pain of the everyday, but with an eternal gleam of heaven in their eyes. They themselves could now be stars in the nights of others. Paul tells the Corinthians that, once changed by God's revelation in Christ, we can go "with our faces shining with the brightness of his face" (2 Cor 3:16).

To belong to Christ is to be back in the battle with him. It's to go into the lost world with a vision of how people can be restored and a hope that sustains even if all seems to be going wrong. The world is that place where God goes even though the divine will is not being done. It's a darkness where the night stars need to be shining as brightly as possible.

Going into the darkness with God requires appreciating the words of Dietrich Bonhoeffer. He spoke them in prison before the Nazis executed him. "Of course, not everything that happens is the will of God, yet in the last resort nothing happens without His will: that is, through every event, however untoward, there is always a way through to God."[92] The way through evil to God is selfless service to others in the name of Christ. It may not be pain free, but it can be pleasure laden. The mourning can lead to morning, darkness to the dawning of joy.

The first chapters of Luke report the Christmas events. The angels sang, the baby was born, the worshipping visitors came, Mary treasured it all in her heart, and then what? The shepherds "returned" to caring for their needy sheep. The coming of Jesus is not the leaving of our responsibilities, however full of amazement we might be. It's returning with a new zest for our sacred responsibilities. The difference is that our steps are now lighter, our pain more bearable, our eyes more focused on the stars.

The disciples of Jesus were very different from each other. Take Nathanael (Bartholomew) and Simon Zelotes. One loved prayer meetings and the other political rallies. One would have gladly stayed on the mountain of transfiguration with Jesus and the other would have left immediately, choosing practical action on behalf of the poor to spiritual contemplation and constant worship. One wanted to focus on the world to come and the other on the world as it is. Which of these men did Jesus call to be his disciple? Both!

They were both right, but each only half right. Jesus embraced both and tried to teach each one the fuller approach to discipleship and mission. The one who was reaching toward God was wrong only when he became so heavenly minded that he no longer was of much earthly good. The one reaching toward the needs of the poor at cost to himself was wrong only when he became so fixed on his social passion and ability to succeed that he lost touch with the gifts and heart of God that should be driving and must be enabling.

There must be no disconnect. Disciples of Jesus must be aglow on the mountaintop with Jesus and shining that light in the dark alleys below—where they also will be with Jesus. The shepherds are to be kneeling before the baby and protecting the baby's little sheep lost in the dangerous valleys of this world. We are to be healed in divine presence and vulnerable in divine service. We are to follow Jesus on a difficult and pain-filled path, loving the world while shunning "worldliness."

We are called to value all people without necessarily adopting their values and goals. We are to give to Caesar only what is his, while working toward wrenching from his control what belongs only to God. We must risk living out the difficult *in-out* paradox. Christian disciples are to be witnessing in this world about the present foretaste and anticipated future of another world outside current ways of being and valuing. Jesus saw his disciples less as a *privileged* group rescued from this world and more as a *commissioned* group with special responsibility for this world.

Albert Schweitzer pointed the right way. He had learned of the great misery in Africa. Could comfortable Europeans be justified in ignoring it just because newspapers preferred to concentrate on other things? Should the "civilized" be satisfied with their privileged blindness? What of the millions in desperate need of the medical help being hoarded by the rich? Assistance with the pain could be made available. Must we not awake and put ourselves at risk? Yes, Schweitzer concluded, and we should know that addressing the pain of others can be a path to joy for ourselves.

Odd Combinations

What odd combinations, suffering and rejoicing, the opaqueness of night and the brightness of the stars, addressing pain and finding joy. Odd or not, the fact is that Christian faith puts them together.

Karl Marx was wrong. Christianity, at least when lived as it should be, is not an opiate that helps people run away from the real world of pain. It actually sends us into the darkness with healing light. Choosing loyalty to God's will, even when it means suffering, is evidence of the maturity of a faithful follower of the Master. Joy trumps pain when we are engaged in loving service to the least among us. In the darkest night are the brightest stars.

When seeing the cross ahead, Jesus did anything but run away from trouble. Suffering had to be faced and a lost world redeemed. His disciples would have to learn that true faith shines forth *especially when it hurts*. Paul said to the Colossians, "I am now rejoicing in my sufferings for your sake, and in my flesh I am completing what is lacking in Christ's afflictions for the sake of his body, that is, the church" (1:24, NRSV). Suffering in the service of redemption; pain that somehow births rejoicing; walking with Jesus to the cross; heading toward a suffering that soon will yield resurrection—it's all the jagged and joyous journey of Christian faith and life.

The odd combination of suffering and rejoicing is possible when a faithful disciple of Jesus is afflicted unjustly. James Macholtz, a sports coach friend of mine, wrote a little book with the unusual title *How to Be a Winning Loser*. Long before that, the psalmist offered a similar promise: "Weeping may stay for the night, but rejoicing comes in the morning" (Ps 30:5). Loss in the world's eyes may be victory on the larger scene.

The cross of Jesus was both the darkness of suffering and the dawning of a bright new day for the whole world. What had been the wooden instrument  of death would become the supreme altar of Christian faith, a symbol of eternal life. The ugly night of crucifixion would morph into the glorious morning of resurrection. Tears of despair would be transformed into shouts of joy. The place of terrible death would forever be remembered as the birthplace of life eternal. Deep night was revealing shining stars. What had seemed a tragic end would turn out to be a most wonderful beginning. So it was—and still can be.

To follow this surprising, suffering, dying, and ever-living Jesus requires becoming like him in his humility and self-giving. Winning in life will be found along the jagged path of vulnerable loving. To be holy is to be open to hurt, and in the process it is to become aware of a joy unspeakable. The darkest nights display the brightest stars.

Loss—look out for it! We all will see it come in one form or another. It begins when we are pushed out of the safety of the womb, and it never seems to end until we finally quit the rhythm of breathing. That's the inevitable pain. Here's the possible pleasure. Jesus said, "For those who want to save their life will lose it, and those who lose their life for my sake will find it" (Matt 16:25). The jagged journey is the path through the loss of selfishness to the gain of Christ-likeness.

The ancient prayer of Jabez stretches beyond the pain to the possibility. His Jewish mother gave him a name meaning "pain" (1 Chr 4:7–10). Once grown, Pain called on God to bless him and enlarge his territory so that he could stop the cycle of misery by blessing more and more others. Jabez wanted released from selfishness and ushered into a larger territory where he would have more room to love. Rather than another conveyor of pain, he wanted to be a source of joy.[93] Where pain abounds, God's grace can much more abound.

Our pain can move to praise, loss to laughter, dark nights to bright stars, salty tears to streams of living water. God, so Jesus revealed, is the Suffering Servant and also the Lord of lords and King of kings. Provided for us who believe is an available holiness in this life that centers in an overcoming love reigning in the heart. Such love stabilizes our walking so that suffering is not denied or seen as a dead end. In fact, it comes to be seen as a channel to blessing.

Those perfected in love hardly seek pain or volunteer for martyrdom, but neither do they flee in fear when such things come along as part of the jagged journey. Pain is part of the Christian vocation. To suffer on behalf of the mission of Christ is "the pain of cleaving to faith in him in the midst of an alien world and doing so without pigheadedness, proselyting, or a martyr complex."[94] Why is there pain in this world? The New Testament seems to answer, "Don't ask why. Embrace pain in the service of Christ as your glad vocation."

> Our pain can move to praise, loss to laughter, dark nights to bright stars, salty tears to streams of living water. God is the Suffering Servant and also the King of kings.

The key is compassion, an active entering into the larger community of suffering. We must allow others to help carry our pain, and then reach out to carry the pain of others. That's the painful path to the healed and holy life in which "mourning and dancing are part of the same movement of grace. Somehow, in the midst of your tears, a gift of life is given."[95]

The message of the New Testament is that the holy lives of Jesus' followers will be wonder-full, even if not pain free. To be holy is to choose the path of downward mobility that ends on a cross, and ironically is also the path of upward mobility to resurrection and eternal life. Don't fear the night. Look to the stars.

10

MANAGING THE JOURNEY

How Can I Find Pleasure in Pain?

We had a financial advisor help us understand retirement planning. He called himself a "wealth manager." We certainly didn't think of ourselves as wealthy. On the other hand, we did understand that what little we have should be managed well. That's responsible stewardship. To not plan is to plan badly.

Anything that God [uses to take] you *to* God also will help you *through*. "Rather than ask God to change your circumstances, ask him to use your circumstances to change you."[96]

We humans are all on a trip from a cradle to a grave. Since we can't escape this mortal pilgrimage, can we at least manage it well? It won't be easy. What happens when the jagged journey of faith finds us alone, hurting, seemingly abandoned even by God? How can we manage such a time? How can we be good stewards of what little we have?

Elijah, a rugged man of God, nearly quit. The scheming Ahab and Jezebel had driven him to the point of spiritual collapse. He crawled under a juniper bush to wallow in despair (1 Kgs 19:4). And he's certainly not the only one. Even so, suffering can be managed in ways other than crawling under something and waiting to die. Christianity stands on the foundation of the Jewish tradition that managed to survive a suffering journey throughout much of recorded human memory. Here's a glance at how they managed.

First, Judaism holds that God is with us when we suffer. "Fear not," says the prophet Isaiah, "for I am with you. Be not frightened, for I am your God; I strengthen you and I help you" (Isa 41:10). Second, Judaism sustains those who suffer through maintaining strong bonds of community. Visiting the sick and comforting those in mourning are religious obligations. We are on this mortal trip together. Finally, Judaism copes with suffering by sustaining hope. The story of the Exodus stands as the archetype. Suffering will not have the last word. Slavery eventually gives way to freedom. The long history of Jewish faith and experience has shown it to be so.

Opening keynotes for managing suffering, then, are (1) having a sturdy hope that is (2) sustained by a supportive and remembering community of faith and is (3) enhanced by the assurance that God is present in the midst of it all and intends that good prevail. These keynotes do not answer all questions or necessarily bring immediate relief. What they do is form a sturdy base from which at least to begin the management process.

The Key Is Hope

The prophet Jeremiah had been a bold spokesperson for God, but the day came when his sermons made him a public joke (Jer 20). He soon came to the end of his rope, was sick of the ridicule, and nearly turned in his prophetic credentials. "Speak for yourself, God. It hurts too much for me to do it anymore!" He cursed the day he was born. Life had been mostly trouble and tears, and the future looked like nothing but more of the same (Jer 20:18). Have you ever been there?

How did abused prophets like Jeremiah manage to go on? The same way Jesus did when he was facing the terrible circumstance of betrayal and arrest. He prayed and an angel responded, this time face up in a garden instead of face down under a bush (Luke 22). Whatever we think of angels, this much can be said for sure. Messages from God somehow get carried between worlds, God's and ours. And the angelic word to us in our despair is one of promised strength in times of distress. "The Lord is the strength of my life; of whom shall I be afraid?" Do you hear this divine message that's heavy with hope? It will make the difference so needed.

We can choose to hear an angel's voice while in our painful place of desperate prayer. If we do, then we can get up and go on, even if it's to a cross. If we hear, and manage to get up and go on, it's only because we have come to have hope and know this:

> I cannot do without Thee!
> > I cannot stand alone;
> I have no strength nor goodness
> > nor wisdom of my own.
> But Thou, beloved Saviour,
> > art all in all to me,
> And perfect strength in weakness
> > is theirs who lean on Thee.[97]

Sometimes animals seem better at this than people. Consider donkeys and sheep. Since God made humans verbal beings at creation, why not a donkey when his brutal master wasn't seeing the obvious? Here's a new twist on speaking in tongues. The story is found in Numbers 22. Balaam looked straight at an angel in the road with an important message from God and could see only his stubborn donkey—who did realize what was going on.[98] To be fair to old Balaam, if you had been standing at the foot of the cross watching the brutal murder of Jesus, would you have realized how God was wonderfully reaching toward you in love? Probably not.

> If we can hear an angel's voice while in our painful place of prayer, we can get up and go on, even if it's to a cross.

When it comes to intelligence, sheep apparently rank rather low. However, when it comes to carriers of biblical texts, for a long time they ranked right at the top. One copy of the Gutenberg Bible is said to have required the skins of about 300 sheep. A poet has mused over this and pictured a holding pen of that many sheep behind an old stone building housing one of those famous presses. He tried to enter the thinking of a particular woolly one about to be turned into a page on which ink could be pressed with holy writ.

Pondered the poet, "there is no telling which one will carry the good news that the Lord is a shepherd."[99] In dying, the sheep's very back would soon carry the good news. Likewise, we who yield to God's re-creation can die to ourselves and then live as carriers of God's personal love message to the world. Even with all our limitations, we can manage and become communicators of God's good news. Even in death, we live!

Jürgen Moltmann was certainly an unlikely pick of the sheep for carrying Psalm 23 on his back. In 1943 his high school class was conscripted as auxiliaries for Hitler's air force. Soon he was standing on a gun emplacement in Hamburg, Germany, just as the Allies unleashed Operation Gomorrah, a mass bombing of the city intended to break morale and incite rebellion against the Nazis. A friend standing nearby had his head blown off. Jürgen survived and spent the next five years as a prisoner fighting dirt, lice, and sickness. Late in those years, surely by God's grace, he found himself in a Scottish prison. Moltmann was given a Bible by a chaplain, and Norton Camp became a monastic existence where this brilliant young man was privileged to live an intense intellectual and growing spiritual life.

What was the result of this time of forced isolation, study, and searching? The searcher was found! "In the darkest pit of my soul, Jesus sought me and found me." Within a few years this boy soldier would emerge back in devastated Germany as an intellectual leader of the Christian community worldwide. He would initiate a "theology of hope" movement in Christianity. From Gomorrah arose the kingdom of God. Moltmann reports, "I went through my life with increasing gratitude. After those early experiences of death, life has for me always been a wonderful alternative, and every morning a surprise to be welcomed."[100]

Jeremiah's depression was overcome and he still speaks today. The Moltmann journey is an amazing story of God's grace bringing hope in the worst of circumstances. A donkey could see the angel when Balaam couldn't. A sheep, even though slaughtered, became a superb bearer of God's good news for all to see. They all traveled a jagged path leading from pain to joy, devastation to hope, silence to being communicators of God's good news. That's the path that Jesus pioneered and provides. We can manage if we stay on his path since he's "the Way."

Show Up at Rehearsal

To manage the jagged faith journey, you'll have to show up regularly at rehearsal. Your voice must be prepared to express your new hope. Whatever is going on, don't forget to sing. The quality of your voice isn't the issue; the issue is your determination to connect with divine resources and witness to divine possibilities. If your heart hopes to beat with the richness of the Hebrew spiritual heritage, you have a standing invitation to join the psalmist's choir. Its rehearsal schedule includes working on songs to meet every mood and life circumstance you will ever face.[101]

Psalm 116 shares the testimony of a grateful man anxious to make a thank offering of rejoicing for God's goodness to him. Being saved by God from some awful trouble, he now was enjoying the presence of God's people in the courts of Jerusalem's great Temple. But what if the trouble had persisted and the people were scattered and the Temple destroyed? What happens to salvation songs when no salvation comes? What of the painful silence when God seems to be on an extended and heartless vacation, when singing has been drowned out by suffering?

Psalm 137:4 asks these difficult questions amid agony. It was a particularly difficult choir rehearsal. How can we sing the Lord's song in a strange land? How can suffering servants of God sing the songs of their faith when exiled in alien territory and oppressed by arrogant unbelievers? Many Jews in Babylon had stopped showing up at their faith's choir rehearsals because of deepening despair and growing hopelessness. Why keep practicing for a day that apparently isn't coming?

Despite all, some did keep showing up. They deliberately worked at keeping their memories and dreams alive through the beauty of sacred song. They sang right into the teeth of their pain. Some dared to sing as a way of showing Babylon that their spirit hadn't been broken and their dreams hadn't died. The Jews had been warned that after entering their promised land they must never forget how they managed to get there (God's gift). To forget would lead to disaster (Deut 6:10).

These are the lyrics of treasured memory and determined defiance often voiced by Jews under stress: "Lord God of hosts, be with us yet, lest we forget, lest we forget." To manage their suffering, they had to keep remembering, stay active in the supportive community of faith, and have their faith nurtured through singing the community's songs of enduring hope.

James Stewart points to those who, even when "nailed to some little cross, with the nails running like hot agony through their souls, can cry, 'Hallelujah' . . . even *there* and even *then!*"[102] Recall Jesus in that Upper Room with enemies standing outside the door. He shared a sacred time of encouragement with his disciples and then, *when he had sung a hymn*, went out. His departure was covered with memory, defiance, and doxology. He walked toward the waiting lions wrapped in a sacred song of his community of faith. Fresh notes of memory and rhythms of hope radiated through his very being.

Those exiled Jews before Jesus' time had been promised a return to Zion and with it a fresh song of joy in the midst of their pain. "The ransomed of the Lord shall return and come to Zion with songs and everlasting joy upon their heads" (Isa 35:10). Isaiah 52:9 had put the hope plainly and paradoxically by pairing ruins and joy: "Burst into songs of joy together, you ruins of Jerusalem, for the Lord has comforted his people, he has redeemed Jerusalem." Song is possible even in the face of devastation. Pain, when surrounded by hopeful song and shared with believing sisters and brothers, can be managed even when returning to ruins.

Peter calls his readers to focus on God's salvation in Christ, and "in this you will greatly rejoice." He then adds, "though now . . . you have had to suffer grief in all kinds of trials" (1 Pet 1:6–7). Faithful followers of Jesus can rejoice in their salvation even as they suffer deep grief, hurt, and sadness. The people of Jesus can be in deep trouble and at the same pulsate with vibrant rejoicing. Pain can be managed by pairing it with remembering and rejoicing.

Tears as Telescopes

Tears can be viewed in various ways. When first dating my wife, I found that she cried easily. She assured me that I should not to be distracted by this. She has a quick "on button" for tears. Her emotions are close to the surface. This is both her glory and sometimes her awkwardness. It's just her temperament. Tears are beautiful, pathetic, upsetting, comforting, and sometimes confusing.

Tears can be hard to read. Take the prophets Amos and Hosea. One thundered at the guilty with a trumpet while the other wooed the lost with a tongue of sheer beauty. The first was an announcer of doom on God's wayward people. They hadn't cried in repentance when they should have; now God would take them out with a blank face! The second didn't deny that God could be the judge when necessary. He chose instead to focus on the tear in God's eye. "Israel, how can I give you up?" (Hos 11:8). God is power, but the greatest perfection of the Divine is love. God has tears, some expressing grief and some joy.

When people cry, it's easier to see right into their very souls. Tears can be telescopes. It's the same with God. Often it's "in the shadows of some dark valley that the soul discovers how near God is and how marvelous his all-sufficient grace."[103] When looking at the cross of Jesus, we can be paralyzed with sorrow or propelled with joy. That cross is the worst of human doing and also the best of divine revelation.

Why has that little hill of Golgotha, place of the skull, become the center of the spiritual world? Because that's the place of revelation where the guilt that breaks our hearts met the God whose sacrificing love is dramatized and passes all understanding. Tears are telescopes that bring the sight of God's heart much clearer to our searching souls.

What are we doing with our sin beyond destroying ourselves and others? Just this. We're wounding the God who absorbs our wrongdoing with pain and patience. Jesus, God with us in the flesh, is pictured standing on the brow of Olivet. Looking across the valley at the beloved Jerusalem, he is shedding tears because of its sin and God's great love for the sinners.

Hundreds of years earlier, the prophet Hosea's own tears had become telescopes peering right into the heart of God. This tender prophet had learned about the heart of God that pulsates with love. That heart causes many of us to sing the lyrics of George Matheson, "O Love that will not let me go! . . . O joy that seekest me through pain." We can manage our suffering by acknowledging and receiving such love and joy.

> The exiled Jews kept their dreams alive through sacred song. They sang right into the teeth of their pain, showing Babylon that their dreams hadn't died.

The scenes at deathbeds and in funeral homes are usually filled with tears. They're natural expressions of grief, but they can be even more. They can be telescopes that see far beyond the immediate sorrow and loss. They can glimpse the eventual triumph of God. They can know a love and joy leading toward eternal victory.

One winter evening, Thomas Hardy walked aimlessly in the fields. Everything seemed to him bleak and dismal and dead. Life had taken leave of him. Then, from a tree high above, a bird burst into a song of joy, causing the poet to wonder:

> I could think there trembled through
> His happy good-night air
> Some blessed Hope, whereof he knew
> And I was unaware.

And there's this prayer of the ancient psalmist (126:4-6):

> And now, God, do it again—
> Bring rains to our drought-stricken lives,

So those who planted their crops in despair
Will shout hurrahs at the harvest,
So those who went off with heavy hearts
Will come home laughing, with armloads of blessing.

How can we mere humans manage the cutting edges of our jagged faith journeys? We must look up, hear, become aware, and believe that there is a great love that will not let us go, no matter how things seem at present. That love puts a sweet song on the dark night air and releases showers of nurturing water needed for a great harvest. Our drought-stricken lives, planted in despair, can be harvested with armloads of blessing.

Call in the Reinforcements

When suffering comes, there is the constant question *why*. A big part of why's answer is found in 2 Corinthians 1:3–4. In these few lines Paul uses the word *comfort* five times. His meaning goes well beyond mere sentimentalism. The Greek word *paraklesis* is used repeatedly to mean "call in the reinforcements." We get the English word from the Latin *con-fortis*, the elevation of strength, becoming surrounded by a protecting presence. The "God of all comfort" is what Paul calls the arrival of life's greatest support system. We can become strong with the overwhelming strength of God. We can manage when comforted by the divine presence.

Strength to survive suffering is available and makes managing it possible. But why would we want to become strong so that more suffering can be endured? It's a mission answer. We are comforted in our weakness and misery *so that we can comfort others*, "so that we can comfort those in any trouble with the comfort we ourselves receive from God" (2 Cor 1:4). We are saved to serve, healed to heal, strengthened to strengthen, comforted to comfort.

Suffering is transformed only when the suffering of others is addressed with compassion. We become wise only when we are willing to become what the world judges a "fool." That's how the story of the crisis on the Sea of Galilee goes in Matthew 14. The early church preserved and cherished this amazing story of Jesus and Peter because it was about to be swept itself into the deep at any minute by the ugly social waves surging all around.

The issue then and now is bigger than whether or not Jesus controls nature and is a miracle man beyond the belief of modern people. It gets at the very heart of Christian faith. If Jesus says, "Come," dare I be a fool and come, walk right into the apparent impossible, hoping somehow to survive (1 Cor 4:10)? Maybe the typical way that God works is not so dramatic and shocking as th e story of the stormy sea. But what if it should be in my case, in your case? Can the Lord be trusted to provide whatever resources are necessary?

If you ever do hear "Come," can you be sure that it's the Lord doing the inviting? Peter was sure it was Jesus, so he stepped out of the boat and right into the churning abyss. The others in that sinking boat likely thought they were seeing and hearing some evil spirit lurking in the fury and beckoning them to their doom, and that Peter had lost his mind. Of course, we must test the spirits. Especially when we are in pain, there are many voices echoing in our poor heads. Even so, might the true not be standing among the false? Might it really be the Lord?

Did Peter sink into that churning sea? Amazingly, not at first. He was concentrating so hard on Jesus that even the natural world relaxed a moment and forgot to swallow him! Then his attention shifted to the ugly black waters swirling at his feet. What got his attention started to get his body. When we are the "fools" that we should be, divine resources come to our aid. Managing the chaos is successful *only* when Jesus is our preoccupation and all our steps are "for Christ's sake" (1 Cor 4:10). Jesus calls us to do the impossible in this world. We can't, *unless* it's Christ who is doing it through us.

Managing spiritual storms comes down to our answers to these core questions. Do we think we can escape suffering? Should our focus be on escaping or believing? Are we willing to be fools for Christ? Is Jesus our sole preoccupation? Are we willing to enter into the sufferings of Jesus? Are we aware of the basic principles for managing the jagged journey of faith?

Basic Management Principles

As we've already explained, 2 Corinthians 12 is a great place to learn about the *8-9-10* path of the Christian's jagged journey of faith. Now we call attention to 2 Timothy as a great place to find the basic principles for managing this precarious and precious journey.

The focus of Paul's writing to Timothy does not fall on the sicknesses and disasters that tend to happen to us humans just because we live in fragile bodies in a fallen world. That's the common experience of believers and nonbelievers. Rather, Paul is concerned with the particular experience of suffering that comes to followers of Jesus because of their faithfulness to a way of life that is resisted by the world. Here are the seven management principles found in this little letter to Timothy.

> Principle #1—Be aware that suffering has been and can be survived. Timothy had been "a good apprentice" of Paul and had seen firsthand his sufferings in Antioch, Iconium, and Lystra (3:10–11). He also knew Paul's dramatic witness: "God rescued me! Anyone who wants to live all out for Christ is in for a lot of trouble; there's no getting around it." While there's no avoiding it, there are ways of surviving trouble and even channeling it for good. Therefore, be ready "to take your share of suffering for the Message" (1:8). As you do, be confident that all hardships can be survived. Timothy had seen Paul survive. Testimonies of past saints are resources for those who must yet endure suffering for the Master.

Suffering is transformed only when the suffering of others is faced with compassion. We become wise only when we are willing to become what the world judges a "fool."

> Principle #2—Know that you can't make it on your own. There should be no shame or fear in witnessing for the Lord, and even of being identified with Paul who was in prison for his witness. "We can only keep on going, after all, by the power of God, who first saved us and then called us to this holy work" (1:8). Self-sufficient disciples are self-deceived disciples. Only the grace of God will be adequate when the pain comes.

> Principle #3—Focus on the only reason for being confident. If we can't count on our own resources, what can we count on? It had been difficult for Paul, but he had come through his trials with head high and no regrets, even though he was in prison. How did he manage that? Because "I couldn't be more sure of my ground—the One I've trusted in can take care of what he's trusted me to do right to the end . . . . Since the appearance of our Savior, nothing could be plainer: death defeated, life vindicated in a steady blaze of light, all through the work of Jesus" (1:9–12). If life can survive death when faithfully related to Jesus, Timothy and we have every reason to be confident no matter the circumstance. Don't doubt in the dark what you've seen in the light.

Principle #4—Be diligent as Jesus was. Don't be tempted by shortcuts and offers of an easier way. Don't be distracted by the trivia of everyday affairs. Keep your eyes on the demanding task. "When the going gets rough, take it on the chin with the rest of us, the way Jesus did. A soldier on duty doesn't get caught up in making deals at the marketplace. He concentrates on carrying out orders. An athlete who refuses to play by the rules will never get anywhere. It's the diligent farmer who gets the produce" (2:3-6). The quitter is always the loser. Jesus endured even the cross on his way to ultimate victory. Stay the course and one day you can claim the prize.

Principle #5—Avoid being naïve. Never kid yourself. "There are difficult times ahead. As the end approaches, people are going to be self-absorbed, money-hungry, self-promoting, stuck-up, profane, contemptuous of parents, crude, coarse, dog-eat-dog, unbending, slanderers, impulsively wild, savage, cynical, treacherous, ruthless, bloated windbags, addicted to lust, and allergic to God. They'll make a show of religion, but behind the scenes they're animals. Stay clear of these people" (3:1-5). Timothy surely was warned, and so are we. "You're going to find that there will be times when people will have no stomach for solid teaching, but will fill up on spiritual junk food—catchy opinions that tickle their fancy. They'll turn their backs on truth and chase mirages" (4:3-4). Don't be surprised or disheartened. Absorb the abuse for resisting such times and people.

Principle #6—Lean on God's revealed Word. A dependable flow of wisdom is available in tough times. "There's nothing like the written Word of God for showing you the way to salvation through faith in Christ Jesus. Every part of Scripture is God-breathed and useful one way or another—showing us truth, exposing our rebellion, correcting our mistakes, training us to live God's way. Through the Word we are put together and shaped up for the tasks God has for us" (3:16-17). Soaking up the wisdom of God equips us for the hard times.

Principle #7—Know that only God has the final say. Temporary setbacks are likely, but they're not the point. "Christ himself is the Judge, with the final say on everyone, living and dead. He is about to break into the open with his rule, so proclaim the Message with intensity; keep on your watch" (4:1-2). The return and final victory of Jesus are just over the horizon. We are called to be faithful *in the* *meantime.* "Keep your eye on what you're doing; accept the hard times along with the good; keep the Message alive; do a thorough job as God's servant" (4:5).

There they are, the seven basic principles for the management of suffering and success as Christ's representative. Be faithful. The journey can be completed with rejoicing. Being true to these principles, however, involves more than determining to follow them. It requires intentional training for Christ-likeness.

THE FACT IS

Weakness Can Be Strength
(2 Cor 12:10)

11

TRAINING FOR CHRIST-LIKENESS

Shortcuts Are Not Allowed

We also boast in our sufferings, knowing that suffering produces endurance, and endurance produces character, and character produces hope, and hope does not disappoint us, because God's love has been poured into our hearts through the Holy Spirit that has been given to us (Rom 5:3–5).

He comes to us as One unknown, without a name, as of old by the lakeside he came to those men who knew him not . . . . To those who obey him, he will reveal himself in the toils, the conflicts, the sufferings that they will pass through in his fellowship and, as an ineffable mystery, they will learn in their own experience who he is.[104]

Becoming like Christ is a combination of two things. Suffering is at the base of both. One involves being emptied of our self-preoccupation in favor of being filled with God's Spirit. The other is spending quality time with Christ in the routines of our living, learning through harsh experience who he really is and who we can be when really living in him. Elsewhere I picture this process of becoming like Christ as a submerged swimmer racing toward the water's surface to refill lungs with life-giving oxygen. It's the process of "exhaling death and inhaling life."[105]

The goal of this demanding process is gaining the mind of Christ for ourselves. "Let this mind be in you that was in Christ Jesus" (Phil 2:5). My friend Clark Pinnock put it well: "The body of Christ no longer denotes only the physical existence of Jesus but is a corporate term referring to the community on its way to Christ-likeness."[106] That community is the church, disciples together on their way to reflecting the character and joining the mission of Jesus today.

This reflecting and joining will be a struggle since we are fallen beings who remain vulnerable to the pull downwards, the temptation to be very unlike Christ. To invite the reign of God into one's life is to be on the journey of becoming "holy" as God is holy. This involves yielding intentionally to a gracious invitation upward. The rich young ruler wanted to be holy, asking what else was necessary to get there, but he balked when Jesus told him to give up his riches (Luke 18:18–23). Isn't there some way that doesn't cost? Apparently not. No shortcuts are allowed. Sacrifice and suffering are essential.

Emptied and Filled

There's no shortcut to the best of all destinations, being so filled with Christ's Spirit that we actually become like Christ in character and function like Christ in our living. One cost is the pain involved in being willing to change. Religious people who are convinced that they have a corner on truth may be the most resistant to change. Unfortunately, "this resistance to change is so common that it is almost what we expect from religious people who tend to love the past more than the future or the present."[107]

Are you ready to yield and change, exhale and inhale? Be warned. Like anything else, being transformed, gaining the mind of Christ, growing into spiritual maturity is not a simple matter of instant gratification gained by using holiday discount coupons passed out in church. It will take time, intentionality, and all we have.

The song "River God" by Nichole Nordeman imagines each of us as rough stones being slowly rubbed smooth by the ever-rushing water that is the ongoing work of God. The composer sees herself as "a stone rough and grainy still, trying to reconcile this river's chill." She knows that "time brings change and change takes time." Her prayer is that one day God might pick her up "and notice that I am just a little smoother in your hand."

An old Cherokee was teaching his grandson about life. "A fight is going on inside us," he said to the boy. "It's between two wolves, one very good and one very evil." The boy thought about that image and finally responded, "Which one will win?" The simple answer given was, "The one you feed." In other words, be intentional; keep your rough self in God's rushing river; keep feeding the good wolf; grow in Christ-likeness by the smoothing action of God.

There's something necessary for personal transformation, for training in Christ-likeness, something beyond the investment of time and intentionality. It's something hardly welcome. The true identity of Jesus and our becoming like him will happen only through toils, conflicts, and sufferings as we live and grow in fellowship with the Master. Training for Christ-likeness involves pain and suffering as well as time and work.

> Being filled with Christ's Spirit, we actually become like Christ in character and actions. That's "holiness," Jesus Christ in us.

There will be some jaggedness to this faith journey. Throughout the ups and downs, much of the outcome will depend of what we choose to feed and allow God to do. Feeding the good wolf will involve focus and cost, and it won't always be comfortable.

"Thank God for pain!" is what Dr. Paul Brand is reported to have once said. For this famous doctor, pain represents God's great gift so desperately needed by the millions of leprosy victims. The loss of feeling is dangerous to the body and soul. To feel is to be warned of danger and treated with pleasure. Lacking feeling as believers in Jesus is to be leprous, unable to really understand, unwilling to really serve, walled off from the wind of the Spirit, numbed to the present work of God in this world, isolated from being truly like Christ.

To feel deeply is to love and gain the ability and motivation to serve selflessly in Christ-like ways. Such service is riddled with risk and infused with joy. It's as necessary as difficult. It's the Christian way. To be perfected in love is to become holy. Such becoming is never instant or painless, but "holiness" is the big subject, the spiritual goal.

Being holy is being like God in this world. Such a lofty goal is far from our reach, we naturally say, and that's certainly right. But here's the key point. Holiness is not about *us* but about *Jesus Christ in us*. He's the embodied image of the holy God who has appeared in this world. Our goal is not to *be* him but "to turn toward him and reflect his image.... We are not a people in need of new strategies for bringing people to Christ; we are a people who need to seek the face of God. It is his radiant glory that will attract people, not to us but to him."[108]

The wise of this world say that holiness is only religious idealism, a state of super-spirituality reserved for the very few and for another life. But the New Testament is much more universal and immediate and optimistic than that, more oriented to the present lives of all believers. There is a path to New Testament holiness. It requires intentionality that centers in yielding. The pain of the loss of self-centeredness is necessary. It's suffering, giving up control, risking the unknown, doing things God's way, appearing foolish in this world.

Paul understood himself to be a servant of Jesus Christ, functioning on behalf of the church, serving *for* Christ and *like* Christ. It was all being made possible because Paul was privileged by God's grace to be living *in* Christ. A Christian is defined by the apostle as *Christ in you*, the hope of glory (Col 1:27). Paul thought of himself as an agent of Christ and a servant of the church.

The apostle clearly was a leader in early church life, but one of the suffering-servant kind (Isa 53). He was prepared to set aside self-interest and the political manipulation of people in favor of submitting to others and sharing their burdens (Gal 6:1–10; Phil 2:1–11). Submission and burden-bearing are key to Christ-likeness, but they come at a price. Suffering often accompanies faithful discipleship.

God freely gave up his Son for the sin of us humans; disciples of the Son are to freely give up themselves in loving service, regardless of the consequences. The church is to be a fellowship of those pouring themselves out for others. How is this possible? It's possible only because Christ's Spirit has been poured into humble believers. "The golden age only comes to men when they have, if only for a moment, forgotten gold."[109] When Christ is the center of attention, flashes of God's golden age streak into us, and then through us to others.

Again, the key word for such difficult forgetting of false gold is *intentionality*. This implies preparation, readiness, having at hand the needed resources. We shouldn't expect instant maturity from those not ready—teenagers? Unfortunately, getting ready for maturity can mean making one's own mistakes and surviving early experiences in life not of our own making. So, as one mature spiritual man has counseled, "do not waste a moment of time lamenting poor parenting, lost job, failed relationship, physical handicap, gender identity, economic poverty, or even the tragedy of any kind of abuse. Pain is part of the deal. . . . All the emptying out is only for the sake of a Great Outpouring. God, like nature, abhors all vacuums, and rushes to fill them."[110]

Ignore Mr. Worldly Wiseman

The first thing I remember my seminary dean saying to us new ministerial students was that the call to preach is the call *to prepare*. Have you ever had that awful dream about arriving at the airport for your big trip and having an attendant tell you that you have no reservation in their system? Have you ever stopped for a quick gasoline fill-up and suddenly realized that you left your wallet or purse at home? Are you willing to face a congregation or the world with only simplistic and thoughtless generalities about the faith?

Recall this dramatic scene from the life of the Apostle Paul. He was on a ship, a helpless prisoner on his way to face Caesar. Luke reports that the ship was caught in a storm and the sailors feared they were approaching land and would be crushed on the rocks. They did the one thing left to do, throw out their four anchors and hope they would catch and avoid the disaster (Acts 27:27–29). Can you hear one frantic sailor suddenly yelling, "We left the anchors back at the last port! We're doomed!" Proper preparation is essential.

It's like that as we go through life. A storm comes up, some kind of suffering, and we fear the worst. Have we prepared for this emergency? Are there resources aboard to meet the danger? What we need can't be bought or borrowed once the crisis has arrived. Help is needed immediately or likely we'll be lost. Can we accept the wisdom of Kahlil Gibran? "Out of suffering have emerged the strongest souls; the most massive characters are seared with scars." Seared, yes, and also surviving if Christ has been nurtured within.

Self-surrender is essential although hardly comfortable and easy. This prayer of John Wesley shows the right way. "I am no longer my own, but yours. Put me to what you will, rank me with whom you will; put me to doing, put me to suffering; let me be employed for you or laid aside for you, exalted for you or brought low for you; let me be full, let me be empty; let me have all things, let me have nothing; I freely and wholeheartedly yield all things to your pleasure and disposal."[111]

Put me to suffering? Not an easy prayer. Facing the challenges of moving through the stages of life, physical and spiritual, will no doubt bring some suffering. No strain and stress, no pain or there'll be moving on. No costly ministry to the despairing, no fellowship with Jesus, no carrying the cross with Jesus, then there'll be no resurrection scheduled for the future.

Shortcuts to spiritual maturity, to holiness, readily present themselves and are tempting. They appear time-saving and more comfortable. Even so, John Bunyan got it right. He has Mr. Worldly Wiseman get poor Pilgrim into deep trouble. He encouraged Pilgrim to take a shortcut to the Celestial City. Pilgrim took it and the result was costly. Growth is not simple. Faith dare not settle for the simplistic. Mature people are not *either-or* thinkers, but bathe in the more complex and realistic ocean of *both-and*.[112]

The world is full of advisors who claim quick routes to getting wherever we like. Self-help gurus are common and flush with appealing promises. Nevertheless, Bunyan's lesson for us pilgrims of faith is simply this. The longest way around may be the shortest way home. Maturing as a Christian believer is hardly a one-shot, quick-fix, overnight business available at discount and postage paid. There's wisdom in the song that calls on us to "take time to be holy."[113] Trying to duck the discipline, avoid the pain, and not take up the cross of Jesus daily is both understandable and self-defeating.

The lyrics of a well-known song by William D. Longstaff call for us to "speak oft with thy Lord, abide in him always, and feed on his Word." We disciples of Jesus are people on the way to becoming more like our gracious Master and Teacher. We must continuously open ourselves to growth and change. Being a real Christian always involves *becoming* while on the way, gaining benefit even from the jaggedness of the journey. The first Christians were called "people of the way." Jesus said that he *is* the way, the means of positive change and also its goal.

What is the "holiness" goal of the Christian's jagged journey? What would we look like if we do manage to get there? Here's the best description I know. "The saint is precisely one who has no 'I' to protect or project. His or her 'I' is in conscious union with the 'I AM' of God. . . . Such people do not need to be perfectly right, and they know they cannot be anyway; so they just try to be in *right relationship*."[114] Being *in Christ* daily is being rightly related, being holy.

Tested and Tempted in Church School

Think of the church as a school for believers in training for engagement with the world. It's a staging ground where teaching and testing and tempting happen. It's the setting where members develop the virtues and skills necessary for serving the world in sacrificial and costly ways. Being thought of this way, a crucial question haunts the church today. Are we cherishing the cross of Jesus as a sacred symbol of faith while also quietly shunning its discipline? Are we lauding its blessings while avoiding its call to pain?

At the center of the biblical story is God's embracing of Israel's pain, caring in costly ways. At the heart of the New Testament is God in Christ embracing the pain of the whole world in the costliest of ways. Can the cross of Jesus be remembered reverently without the church also preparing to embrace the pain of today's world? No. "The way of the Cross provides the model for God's new social order, the messianic community in which suffering servanthood replaces lordship over others. The church becomes the social expression of the way of the Cross."[115]

There's a role for the negative in the perfecting of the positive. Testing and tempting are two "t" words related and yet very different. They will both show up along our faith journeys. The contrast between them is that they come from different sources and arrive with differing intents. Bunyan's Mr. Worldly Wiseman was a tempter. Jesus is a tester. One undermines our becoming in Christ and the other encourages it.

Isaac Watts penned these wonderful lines: "Since I must fight if I would reign, Increase my courage, Lord!" The fight will be against tempting, while there may be struggling involved with testing. So Watts adds: "I'll bear the toil, endure the pain, Supported by Thy Word." Pain may come from two sources and can be endured when one is supported by divine resources.

There will be some walking through fiery ordeals (1 Pet 4:12). It's important to note that a fiery furnace (1 Pet 1:6–7) is what we would call a *forge* where things can be destroyed or shaped, refined, purified, and made more beautiful and honoring to Jesus Christ. Faithful followers are tested in this heat in order that they might rise more in the image of Christ. But they also will be tempted to go a very different way, the way of destruction and not shaping.

Jesus counsels his disciples as any good teacher would his students. Tests are part of the curriculum of the maturing follower of the Lord. God tests to check for integrity and encourage progress. Faith untested can hardly be trusted. It must grow so that it can survive and serve well in a dangerous world, being supported by the promise of Jesus that even this world has been overcome (John 16:33). Classic hymn lyrics put it well. God announces and assures:

> When through fiery trials thy pathway shall lie,
> My grace, all sufficient, shall be thy supply:
> The flame shall not hurt thee, I only design
> Thy dross to consume and thy gold to refine.[116]

Why is this world so dangerous for the Christian? It's because there's more than *testing* along the jagged journey. There's also *tempting*, deliberate seductions from an evil source. The testing prepares one for resisting the tempting. We must be on guard. "Let anyone who thinks that he stands take heed lest he fall" (1 Cor 10:12). The evil one uses even people and events in church life as avenues of possible spiritual destruction. Remember Ananais and Sapphira (Acts 5) and the troublemakers in the Corinthian church (1 Cor 1:4–17, 5:1–6:20)? Whenever possible, evil infiltrates the church and works from the inside (Phil 3:17–21; 2 Tim 3:1–9).

Pain was very real for Daniel S. Warner, an American church reformer, but he found strength to turn it into ministry that blessed others. He suffered from fragile health much of his adult life and was haunted by family tragedies. In 1872 he and his wife Tamzen had triplets. Mother and babies died. Then in 1878 he lost his beloved daughter Levilla Modest when she was only three years old, followed by his second wife turning against his ministry and divorcing him. Despite all, he looked upward in faith and moved on. What could have been temptations leading to disaster were received as testings leading to enhanced divine service.[117]

> Jesus tests his disciples. Tests are part of the curriculum of the maturing follower of the Lord. They check for integrity and encourage progress.

This was the announcement Warner made to a holiness church convention in 1880: "God is looking around for someone he can trust. If God can't get a large vessel, He will take a small one." The question is not our size or strength, education or prominence, but our availability. Isaiah was broken and overwhelmed, but repentant and willing to be sent (Isa 6). Are you? Will you accept your circumstances, even the bad ones, and allow God to shine through the darkness?

TRAINING FOR CHRIST-LIKENESS

Remember that God works for good in the midst of everything, including temptations (Rom 8:28). The question is not, "Have I been knocked down?" It is, "By God's power and my choice, am I getting up and going on?" God is looking for people who can be trusted to share the love of Christ, regardless of circumstances. Is that you?[118] It certainly was Paul.

Check out Colossians chapter four. Paul was faithful to Christ and for that he was slammed in jail. Was he angry, sulking, defeated? Hardly. He gives his Christian friends important advice on how to function when in trouble. Pray! Pray for what? Relief from the unjust circumstance? Removal of all pain? No, pray for open doors. Pray for eyes that stay open, alert, highlighting gratitude, looking for new ways to tell even more people about the marvelous mystery and love of Christ. "Don't miss a trick. Make the most of every opportunity" (Col 4:5).

Paul was telling the Philippians how good it was even in prison. You can't imprison the saving message of God in Christ. "My imprisonment here has had the opposite of its intended effect. Instead of being squelched, the Message has actually prospered." How? Reported Paul with a gleam in his eye, "All the soldiers here, and everyone else too, found out that I'm in jail because of the Messiah. That piqued their curiosity, and now they've learned all about him" (Phil 1:12–13).

More recently, Alexander Solzhenitsyn witnessed to the same experience in his famous *The Gulag Archipelago*: "It was only when I lay there on rotting prison straw that I sensed within myself the first stirrings of good.... I nourished my soul there, and I say without hesitation: Bless you, prison, for having been in my life."

A pastor friend of mine grew up in very difficult circumstances bad enough to ruin anyone for a lifetime. Then I encountered him one morning carrying on his present ministry so sensitively and wisely, affirming everyone around him. I texted to him my personal appreciation, saying that I knew of no one who had transformed personal pain in the past into such highly productive ministry in the present. He responded with great humility and thanks, making the right point. He was hardly the key actor in the transformation. The reweaving God had threaded great grace through his ripped threads and fashioned them into something of new beauty.

Allow rotting straw and prison bars and bad upbringing to become instruments of spiritual growth that radiates the good news of the freedom and joy of living in Christ. Don't fight the circumstance; use it as an instrument of advancement in ministry. Rather than say, "God, *why*?" ask,

"God, *what*?" What can I learn from this experience? What good can come from it? Who is watching and needs to see Christ in me? "Remember today what you have learned about the LORD through your experiences with him" (Deut 11:2). Rather than ask God to change your circumstance, try asking God to use your circumstance to change you and those around you.

I've had friends who have managed their suffering in ways that actually brightened the lives of attending nurses and orderlies, sometimes witnessing well to their faith. One friend, however, avoided pain medication although suffering significantly with advanced cancer. He fought the pain rather than risk drug dependence, even addiction. His doctor finally took charge, scolding and hospitalizing him. The doctor's logic? "Your body is using all its energy fighting the pain instead of helping the healing!" We must not focus excessively on managing our own pain to the exclusion of maximizing our healing witness to others.

Taking strong medication can be an appropriate way of masking pain, keeping it from disabling our functioning altogether. That's most welcome in extreme physical circumstances. But Paul's spiritual point is different. His concern is that we don't merely fight the pain, but also *channel it*. Don't fear and run from persecution and imprisonment. If they come, and you are faithful, God will be faithful in surprising ways. Maybe your guards and tormentors will be the ones impacted more than you!

Fast Properly and Remember Gratefully

How do we get from our selfishness, the pull downward, to the upward goal of Christ-likeness that God so desires for us? How do we benefit from God's gracious testings that help enable the spiritual maturity needed to resist the temptations always coming from below? There are the seven basic management principles explained above. Christians sometimes have added to these a range of "disciplines" that also can be helpful.

C. S. Lewis offers a caution. "Ascetic practices, which themselves strengthen the will, are only useful in so far as they enable the will to put its own house (the passions) in order, as a preparation for offering the whole man to God. They are necessary as a means; as an end they would be abominable."[119] Self-imposed testings can be enabling or disabling, depending.

The discipline of fasting is a great example of how an important Christian discipline can be good and bad, valuable indeed and downright abominable. It's not a practice to be ignored. After all, as much is said about it in the Bible as about giving, and the missionary activity of the church began in Antioch with fasting and prayer (Acts 13:3). Jesus instructs us to use this practice as a means of spiritual deepening, and he also warns us to use it from right motives (Matt 6:16–18). Proceed with caution, but proceed.

Fasting done properly should be seen as a way of gathering spiritual resources, not denying oneself of needed food. It should be an act of *affirmation*, a positive way of waiting on God, "a means by which new life can be released within us. It is a form of self-death resulting in a spiritual resurrection. . . . It should be a willing exhaling of the temporarily distracting so that we can be inhaling fresh winds of the Spirit."[120]

Such intentional denying oneself is like calling a time out. Fasting is routinely setting aside time and space to allow undivided attention to God's presence, purposes, and provisions. Give your digestive system a little rest. Focus on things higher than food. Turn off distractions—TV, smartphone, DVDs, laptop, things that are addictive to millions these days. Abandon them temporarily in favor of enabling quiet communications to and from God.

Fast, yes, but don't ever give up the bread at the table of the Lord. A good meditation for a Lord's Supper service might begin with . . .

> The bread is lifted up
> The bread is blessed and broken;
> It calls us to make the vulnerable,
> The poor and hungry our priority.

Note that blessedness and brokenness are joined and that we are called to be vulnerable. Poverty and hunger should become the occasion for Christian ministry. It's the worst calling forth the best, a momentary giving up for a long-term spiritual gain.

Spiritual practices that stretch toward growth and ministry may involve some pain, but quickly turn into new possibilities. Broken bread should be lifted and transformed into heavenly healing. Testings strengthen so that temptations dissolve. As we kneel in voluntary self-denial, we come to stand taller in gain for ourselves and others. When we hold still and really listen, the voice of God often

> Allow rotting straw or prison bars or bad upbringing to become instruments of spiritual growth and ministry that radiate the good news and joy of living in Christ.

comes to us from others, the saints of yesterday and today. We can hear them when we are focused on listening intently.

One pastor wrote of precious minutes he once spent alone in front of his fireplace. He had reflected on many of the faces of people he had known and ministered to over the years, and some who had ministered to him. Although he allowed his "memory to play among the years,"[121] this was hardly a game of escaping into yesterday. It was a rich enabling for the coming tomorrows.

If we only would stop and pay attention, we would find that all of us have such a parade of faces, living and dead, friends, family, even enemies, people who have made a difference for us. A friend of mine, an exceptional pastor, called his biography *Giants Along My Path*.[122] In my own autobiography, I have expressed gratitude for twelve individuals who impacted me significantly, all assisting the graciousness of that upward pull of God's Spirit.[123] I can't imagine what I would have become without them!

Of course, thinking of all those faces of our past and present brings to mind midgets as well as giants. Some faces haunt us, have disappointed us, even have sought our destruction. We can benefit from them all. As the fire flickers in our fireplaces, there is so much to remember, so much we can learn. An important spiritual task is sorting through the images, speaking words of forgiveness where necessary, being deeply grateful, laughing at ourselves, focusing particularly on the faces that offer wisdom. We should look for the working of God along our pathways and in our relationships, past and present. Managing our memories is one good way of training for Christ-likeness.

The Song of Heaven

How can worship become real, life-changing, a welcome help for our present suffering that leads to more Christ-likeness? We must sing with Charles Wesley, "Let saints on earth in concert sing, with those whose work is done." Can those loved ones now with the Lord see and hear us struggling here on earth? We don't know. What we do know from the report of Revelation 19:4 is that we who are still below can hear a little of the present singing in heaven. To survive our present suffering requires learning the language and joining the song of that heavenly host.

In your pain, and as you worship, listen carefully. Can you hear the "Amen!" and "Hallelujah!" of yesterday's saints? The "Amen" is the "So be it,

Lord." The will of God is yet to be fulfilled here below, but in the perspective of eternity the fullness and completion already are known. Jesus said, "What I do you know not now, but you shall know hereafter" (John 13:7). In the midst of his miseries and unanswered questions, Paul said, "now I know in part, but then . . . " (1 Cor 13:9–12). Can you hear the voices of those now living in the "then" time? "Just and true are all Thy ways, Thou King of saints."

Those already home know and are rejoicing. It's for us who are still in the hard times of not knowing and not yet at home to hear from above and be encouraged. With us in today's darkness is the Shepherd who gathers the little lambs in his arms, especially the injured and frightened ones, and presses them close to his heart. Hearing the song of the saints and feeling the closeness of the Shepherd, we also can sing, even now, believing that soon the night will be as day.

Pray this as you worship and complete your jagged journey: "Amen, my Lord. Despite my hurting, I believe you and will follow you all the way home. I also will serve you without reservation while on the way." This prayer is Christ-likeness in dedication and action. It's a humble acceptance of the message of the letter to the Hebrews: "None of the faithful got all promised—it is all of us together!" (Heb 11:39–40). We serve together, each do our little part, and receive the promise together, finally joining in the fullness of the song of the saints.

Beyond the "Amen," we also can hear the "Hallelujah." On that other shore, all suffering is now swallowed up in gladness. All crying has turned to singing. The root of this constant outburst of joy is the assurance of the victory of God. Christ is risen! Christ sits at the right hand of the Father. We now are fighting an enemy that we are told is already defeated. Knowing of the devil's demise goes far toward managing the pain of the jagged journey.

Only a few years after the book of Revelation was written, the old Polycarp faced martyrdom in Smyrna because of his unrelenting Christ-likeness. He refused to deny his loving Christ, so they burned him alive. When the church recorded what had happened, the glorious words were, "Polycarp was martyred, Statius Quadratus being procons ul of Asia, *and Jesus Christ being King for ever!*" That's both "Amen!" and "Hallelujah!"

12

THORNS CHANGED TO CROWNS

There Is a Way for the Worst to Become the Best!

God doesn't give us what we can handle;
God helps us handle what we are given.

Jesus' resurrection is the beginning of God's new project not to snatch people away from earth to heaven but to colonize earth with the life of heaven.

—N. T. Wright

With God's help, we can handle whatever we face. And what we face is more than temptations that must be overcome. We face the mission of colonizing the earth with the life of heaven. That will not be easy or comfortable, but it's God's expressed will. Necessarily involved will be finding ways to change thorns into crowns.

Our hope roots in the resurrection of Jesus, but even he didn't begin well. He was the poorest of the poor. When he died he had virtually nothing to leave behind, with one significant exception. "Peace I leave with you, My peace I give unto you" (John 14:27). Quite an exception! Recall this prayer of John Greenleaf Whittier:

> Take from our souls the strain and stress,
> And let our ordered lives confess
> The beauty of Thy peace.

Jesus was afflicted with unjust thorns and forced to wear a mocking crown. Even so, he knew and shares with us a great peace that comes from such mocking turning into eternal rejoicing.

Have you received your share of the peace that passes understanding? As you walk a jagged path through this world, trying to do your share of colonizing earth with the life of heaven, can you see that your pain one day will be transformed into a glory not known by the world? The worst can and will become the best. A crown can be made even out of thorns. Jesus' was. Yours can be too.

I was born and went to college in Pennsylvania, the "Penn's Woods" of the Englishman William Penn. Deeply impacted by the Quaker tradition of Christianity, Penn suffered persecution and wrote the classic *No Cross, No Crown* in 1669 while in prison. Given a large tract of land in the Americas by the king as the way of clearing a debt owed to Penn's father, the son founded Philadelphia as the "City of Brotherly Love." He made an agreement of friendship and cooperation with the area Indians that was never broken. Here was an ordered life that found ways to confess the beauty of Christ's peace, receiving thorns that would morph into true crowns.

Faith's Advent Season

When still in the heat of the battle, when the suffering rages, when God's peace hasn't yet washed over you, know this. You are in the Advent season of faith. Christ is not yet born, but the nativity is near and you long for his soon-coming. It's still dark and dangerous, with days full of jaggedness, but the dawn is only minutes away. You're reaching for hope. It's close by, but it still remains a little out of reach. Advent is the coming that's not yet.

This interim time is when the great words of Israel must become your own. May the expected coming of the healing and victorious Lord shoot through your body and swell up in your soul:

> O come, O come, Emmanuel,
> And ransom captive Israel,
> That mourns in lonely exile here
> Until the Son of God appear. . . .
> Rejoice! Rejoice! Emmanuel
> Shall come to thee, O Israel.[124]

The coming Prince of Peace promises us disciples that he will arrive to forge a crown out of our mass of thorny tears and pain.

> Jesus, Thou art all compassion,
> Pure, unbounded love Thou art,
> Visit us with Thy salvation,
> Enter every trembling heart.[125]

The problem of Advent, of course, is that it's hope is still only promise and not yet reality. The challenge is to believe in the dawn when only hints of the light are yet seen. No matter what the present sickness or even impending death, the promise is that dawn is coming and cannot be stopped! Can you believe that? Can you manage in the meantime? Can you keep from becoming depressed and losing all hope until the new day comes? These are the big questions of faith as we journey along the jagged pathway of this life.

Here's a key insight that's an important survival technique. Don't have false expectations that will only bring you more hurt. We all live in an institutionalized world, including belonging to clubs, banks, political parties, nations, and churches. Often they stand for high-sounding ideals and also frequently function to the detriment of numerous individuals, particularly "outsiders."[126] You'll be served and abused by these groups sooner or later. Think otherwise and you're destined to unnecessary pain. Know that you're surrounded by agents with more than your interests at heart. Even churches sometimes serve their own self-interests despite their much higher intentions.

> The worst can become the best. A crown can be made even out of thorns. That was true of Jesus and can be of you too.

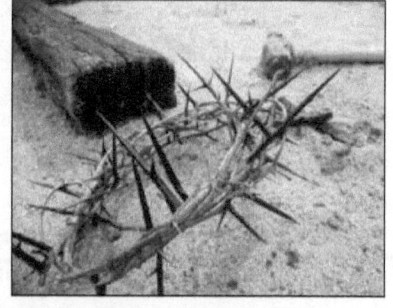

The fact is that a formalized body of any kind is necessarily concerned with achieving and protecting its own identity and interests. It sets boundaries to insure mission success, self-maintenance, self-perpetuation, even self-congratulations. So, belong as you will, participate for the common good, just don't expect that in this world there will be full justice and truly moral behavior on all fronts. To some degree, even if only in subtle ways, you will suffer at the hands of organizations that comprise the webs of your world. Don't be shocked. Be wise and move on. The crown of sainthood has in it many jewels set in holes once made by thorns.

Know one other thing, something very important. The fallenness of this world does have its limits. Pilate once said the most pathetic thing ever to come out of the mouth of a human. The empire he represented was extremely powerful and committed to its own ends, to be sure. It had murdered Jesus and had him buried in a cave-like tomb. Advisers of Pilate were worried that some fanatic Jews would somehow get his body out under the cover of darkness and claim that he was alive again, making him more powerful than the empire itself. Such public trickery couldn't be tolerated. It would cause riots in the streets and displeasure in Rome.

> Pilate told his advisers to "make the tomb of Jesus as secure as you can." Barricading the tomb of God was like shouting "Stop!" to the rising sun.

Pilate responded with super-pathetic words that still ring down the ages. He told his advisers to "make the tomb as secure as you can." That instruction was like shouting "Stop!" to the rising sun or "No!" to the ocean's coming high tide. Poor Pilate ordered his men to barricade the tomb of God! He said pathetically, "Jesus, stay where you are!" He was speaking to the body of Jesus that was destined to resurrection no matter what mere men said or did. The dawning of the Light of the World was inevitable. Poor Pilate.

So, what about your body, a body in pain, one being abused by others and maybe even facing death, clinging to hope in tough circumstances? We're not Jesus, after all. Here's the answer, and it's good news. For all who have a saving relationship to the now-risen Jesus, good is on the way and can't be stopped. For the long term, Jesus promises that he is busy building an eternal home just for us (John 14:3). Whatever happens to our mortal bodies, life and health and divine peace are surely on the way. The Pilates of this world can say and do whatever they want. God always has the last word.

One poet pictures well the real circumstance. He was on a routine country drive when he spotted someone by the roadside just ahead. The strange figure was carrying on his shoulder an enormous scythe. Their eyes met for only a second or two and "voltage ran from my ankles to my scalp." As the figure quickly disappeared behind the car, "I turned off the radio and began to notice how white the houses were, how red the barns, and green the sloping fields."[127] Catching just a glimpse of death can bring fresh breaths of life. A brush with death can be sobering and strangely inspiring. It puts our thorns in perspective and helps us view them as coming crowns.

And here's something else, something wonderful from the Divine Poet. One glance at the empty tomb of Jesus can bring waves of new life! As each new year begins, we tend to make promises to ourselves for doing better than the year now gone. These well-meant but shallow promises usually fall apart within days or weeks. What does not erode into nothing? The gracious promises of God. They stand sure and unchanged regardless of passing time. Can you hear the voice of Jesus? "If I live again, so can you! Since my thorns now comprise a crown, I'm ready to help yours do the same."

One of the most gracious of the promises of Jesus comes in a series of "blesseds," the so-called Beatitudes listed in Matthew chapter five. We are assured by Jesus of the good that absolutely will follow various sufferings that we experience when on the jagged journey of life and faith. The promise of the Beatitudes is that something good will emerge from the dust of something not good. It might not emerge in the way or time we prefer, but we can entrust ourselves to the God who gives special promises to the poor, the widow and orphan, the suffering, the shy, the sorrowful and grieving, those abused by this world, especially those seeking to be faithful to their God.

The Beatitudes present an odd list of promises. Rather than "Blessed are those who are persecuted for righteousness sake, for theirs is the kingdom of heaven," we would choose, "You won't be persecuted since you are always protected by God." Rather than "Blessed are those who mourn, for they will be comforted," we would prefer, "You won't mourn, so no comforting is needed."

We are told to bear each other's burdens as one way of fulfilling the law of Christ. How odd. "Christ came, not to remove life's luggage, but to multiply our burdens.... Christ gives rest to the heart by giving burdens to the shoulders. And, as a matter of fact, it is in being burdened that we usually find rest.... Heavy luggage is Christ's strange cure for weary hearts."[128] The intent of this strange logic is this. We are not promised that there will be no tomb, only that such a place will not be our last residence.

Matthew 5:6 reports this from Jesus: "You're blessed when you've worked up a good appetite for God. He's the food and drink in the best meal you'll ever eat." But even with this promise, those who fear, hurt, and struggle have trouble being sure. It's still only Advent season, not yet the birth scene of fulfillment. Before I manage a good appetite for God, what if I, in my weakness, yield to the temptation to run from the trouble and give up on God?

We live in faith's Advent season, the time of waiting, expecting, not yet having, fearing the trouble, tempted to doubt and run. We are promised a crown but presently are feeling the thorns more than the coming glory. While still in pain, can you hear the first sounds of that joy soon to come? Listen carefully. Pain can be a silencer or a megaphone.

Pain as a Megaphone

We moderns are too busy and short-sighted. We rarely hold still long enough to think deeply and imagine broadly about much of anything. We rarely lie in the grass and ponder the passing clouds, step outside the little box of the immediate and open ourselves to the unknown immensity. To be in awe is to wonder with mouth open, to look beyond what our physical eyes can see. Awe, unfortunately, is now in short supply. There's so much change in today's fast-paced world that we are surprised and impressed by so much, and therefore almost by nothing anymore.

This "numinous" experience of the beyond, the awe in the awesome, is as old as humanity itself. It's at the root of being religious. It finds its fullest development in the great poets, philosophers, and saints. When life-changing insights flood our souls from the large beyond, it could be either supernatural revelation or self-delusion. The person of faith chooses the revelation option. It's always a choice, especially when suffering rages. It's a risk. We could be wrong.

One hears dramatic deathbed reports all the time. Bright lights are spotted at the end of a dark tunnel. Jesus is seen with reaching arms welcoming us home. Pain tends to intensify such experiences. C. S. Lewis said, "God whispers to us in our pleasures, speaks in our conscience, but shouts in our pain; it is His megaphone to rouse a deaf world."[129]

The Bible teaches that God uses suffering to lessen our weaknesses and build up our strengths. Sample passages are Hebrews 12: 1–17; Romans 8: 18–30; 2 Corinthians 1: 3–12, 4: 7–5: 5, 11: 24–12: 10, and nearly all of 1 Peter. How does this work? First, suffering removes blinders and changes our attitude toward ourselves. It humbles us, shows us how fragile we really are, how vulnerable and dependent on God we always have been.

Second, suffering can profoundly change our valuing of some things in our lives. Our titles, accomplishments, contacts, and reputations tend to dissolve quickly when pain comes. Third, and likely most important, suffering can strengthen our relationship to God as does nothing else. We can learn more of God's undeserved compassion toward us and become more compassionate toward others.

Suffering either brings hardness and anger or generates softness and gratitude. It wades in self-pity among the thorns or it finds a way to skip with joy as a new crown is seen being forged. God always makes possible the latter. Pain can sharpen focus on what's most important. But it doesn't always.

That's where the proper point of Lewis has its limit. Dare we think that God uses suffering as an effective, even a typical communication tool? Hear this caution. I can't imagine what sort of message God could communicate through the "megaphone" of the suffering of battered or starving children. How cautious we must be here. Attributing to God's direct action many times sends signals about God that I don't want my megaphone to broadcast.

For example, would God make a husband suffer terribly so that his wife could learn compassion? Would God unleash a terrible disease in order to stimulate a reluctant government to be more generous to its poor? Maybe, rarely.

> Suffering either brings hardness and anger or generates softness and gratitude. It wades in self-pity among the thorns or finds a way to skip with joy as a new crown is being shaped.

It did happen once with the plagues of Egypt and is always possible. Such things, however, remain the exception and hardly reflect the usual manner of Jesus or the prevailing principle that God tends to lead with persuasive love and not manipulative power.

What do you hear from your pain, and where do you see God in life's picture? When great loss comes, is the only voice you hear saying about faith in God, "That was a total waste. So much for my faith and hope!" Are you believing in order to gain special rewards and protections?

A son is highly successful in school and full of idealism before suddenly being killed by a drunk driver. You develop a specialized skill over the years and are poised to move up in the company. Then word comes that your job will be going to another country after your next and last paycheck. Finally, you have become pregnant after years of trying. The birth is glorious and the child perfect. However, at age three the doctor looks at you soberly and announces that there's a brain tumor already beyond control.

Such a colossal waste of life, end of hope, with no more possibilities. Is that all you can hear? Can't you also hear a faint voice saying that it's *not* all waste, not at all. Pieces of the tragedy can be the raw material of an unexpected blessing to you and others. Hearing that voice depends on what you do with your troubles.

Do you brood, concentrate on the negative, or believe that already God is finding ways to transform the negative so that apparent waste can somehow become an unimagined wonder? You feel the thorns stinging. Can you imagine the vision of a crown forming?

The proper Christian reaction to suffering and sorrow is not self-pity or resentment or despair or giving up on God. It's nurturing an attitude of seeing such things as opportunities for fresh and loving divine action. Paul said that in *all things* God works. Every detail in our lives of love for God and service to God can be worked into something good (Rom 8:28). In the lap of love, life's reverses have a way of leaning toward the future.

Here are the right questions to ask when in crisis. How, with God's help, might my awful pitfall become a stepping-stone? How can I receive the trouble as a sacred trust? How can I wear the thorn as an emerging crown? How can my pain become a megaphone of good news, not one of God acting oddly, even heartlessly? Stories are legion of tragedy being turned into triumph.

"Our God is a suffering God," preached Dietrich Bonhoeffer in 1934 as Europe edged toward a terrible war. Those who belong to Jesus "are summoned to share in God's suffering at the hands of a godless world." He wrote these words from Berlin's Tegel Prison. Soon he would be hanged by the Nazis for conspiracy against Hitler. That suffering, in Bonhoeffer's view, is more than the general suffering that comes from being fragile humans in this twisted world. It's "Christian" suffering, the pain coming from voluntarily carrying the burdens of others, pain endured for the sake of Christ. It's suffering because of the promptings of Christ's Spirit (Gal 6:2). It's finding a path through tragedy to the door of triumph.

A friend of mine was the chief executive officer of a large Christian body. Then things went wrong. There was conflict over controversial policies and a breakdown of key relationships. He resigned his leadership position in pain and confusion. Soon came an amazing dream, a divine visitation. Jesus said to him, "I know you want to know what's on the horizon of your life. I want you to make Me your horizon. If you will follow where I lead, I will give you the light needed for your walking into the future."[130]

My friend did make Jesus the center and went on, prompted by Christ's Spirit, to found a new Christian mission organization that now ministers wonderfully to thousands of AIDS orphans in several African nations. Thorns can be melted into crowns when Jesus is made the subject. He then is freed to pioneers a path into tomorrow that is lined with blessings.

One important meaning of the cross of Jesus is that our suffering is also experienced by God. The thorns thrust into the Master's scalp were transformed into a crown for him and us. It now is our turn. Accepting thorns on behalf of others is to have Christ formed in us. He begins to live his ongoing life through us and is crowned anew by our faithfulness. God's life and ours are interactive. Because Christ lives, we too can live!

A secret to surviving suffering is offering the loss we experience on the altar of God right alongside the great sacrifice of the cross of the Master. Dare to make your suffering your offering to God, asking that somehow it be transformed from the ugly into something beautiful, extending Christ's healing ministry through you to someone else.

Yesterday No Measure of Tomorrow

Recall that the life and death of Jesus is a dramatic example of violent and wholly undeserved loss. Despite being God with us, the Creator visiting the creatures, Jesus endured the poorest of lives and worst of ends. Born for a throne, he was hung on a cross. Why this awful waste? How strange and different are the ways of God.

But was it really a waste? Two millennia later, this lonely and abused Galilean is still drawing the whole world to his feet and inspiring in humanity the highest of its potential. The cross was an awful end, but actually more of a wonderful beginning. Consider this. "Let the Cross and Resurrection tell us that the most apparent waste . . . can be the road to life and to the coming of the glory of the Lord!"[131]

Can you envision the possibility that your own loss and suffering has the potential of being a source of fresh good. A special new day can dawn not in spite of but *because of* the difficult road you have had to walk? Every pastor knows that ministry to the grieving rises to a new level when the minister has first suffered loss in his or her own life. Having been there oneself makes possible the careful guidance of a new traveler in the now-known dark valley.

It's a simple fact often seen. Failure and suffering are great levelers among humans. Community can form quickly around suffering. How sad that it takes a grief situation to generate deep solidarity in a family that has been dysfunctional for years. Hospice workers bond with their clients in holy ways.

I recently spent a day in a waiting room while a family member of mine was having brain surgery. I had meaningful conversations with four people doing the same for folks who were total strangers to me. We easily crossed big cultural divides to link in a community of waiting. Pain brought new possibilities of deep understanding and mutual encouragement.

Does yesterday have to define tomorrow? One of the more instructive stories in the Bible is found in chapter two of Zechariah. The awful Exile was finally over for the Jews. The suffering was fading a little at last. Now came the question of how the future should be faced. A young Jewish man is seen roaming around the ruins of Jerusalem. He is measuring the old foundations so that the place can be rebuilt exactly as it once had been. It was to be a fortress against more suffering in the future, a reclaiming of the past, a locking in of wonderful memories.

> The proper Christian reaction to suffering is not self-pity, resentment, despair, or giving up on God. It's seeing pain as an opportunity for fresh divine action. God works in *all things*.

Then something very unexpected happened. An angel intervened and stopped the process. The divine message? The past must not be allowed to define and dictate the future. The Jerusalem of tomorrow was to be a city without walls. God is known by actions in our history, but is never trapped in and forced to repeat yesterday. God is on the move in changing times, and with changes in mind. God's people are to be flexible, honoring the past without the need to repeat it slavishly in new times and places.

The suffering of yesterday must not be allowed to swallow the big possibilities of tomorrow. Out of the ashes of a terrible fire can arise things quite unexpected. "I live," announced Paul, "and yet not I, but Christ who lives in me" (Gal 2:20). Can you measure that? Can life lived in that amazing way be limited to what losses landed on us yesterday? Look at what the carpenter Jesus made out of the wood of his own cross. What might he help you make out of your aloneness, grief, and frustration? Whatever the new may be, it will be different from the old Jerusalem, good as that might have been in some ways.

The dilemma is seen in the labor of love of John Harris. He was a joint organizer of the celebrated 1974 "Destruction of the Country House" exhibition at the Victoria and Albert Museum in London. Many of these "houses" were once palatial estates that had served as safe places for thousands of English children fleeing London in the terrible bombing of World War II. By 1974, however, they were crumbling, abandoned, waiting agonizingly for their ignoble end. Time had passed them by. Many were actually gone (or looked like they should be) by 1998 when Harris completed his book *No Voice from the Hall*. It pictures his nostalgic visits to these once-proud relics of yesterday.[132]

The television phenomenon *Downton Abbey* (2013–2016) was another attempt to look back and remember an earlier time of the English elite, a time that was shown struggling to survive rapid social changes. The persistent question is this: What about yesterday's relationship to tomorrow? Memories and ways of acting are important and hold key lessons. They also must be adapted to a new day. Tomorrow cannot be contained in the limits of yesterday. Jesus said that "no one pours new wine into old wineskins. If he does, the new wine will burst the skins, the wine will run out and the wineskins will be ruined" (Luke 5:37).

Does my suffering dictate my tomorrows? Can a new day be truly new for me? One African American song captures well the power and joy of the social vision of all beleaguered people. It's "a new world a-coming!"[133] Beyond sin, pain, discrimination, and slavery is coming the shalom of God, a hope most available to those particularly mistreated in this world. As an analyst of black preaching has wisely observed, "the congregation can celebrate in advance, and such celebration can be socially dynamic as Christians begin to live freely according to the patterns of life in God's new order."[134]

Tomorrow should be and can begin today! If paradise is our goal, we can be enabled to begin practicing paradise life now, even in our suffering. We are redeemed not *from* the world but *for* it. Ministry can and should emerge from misery. Why should the church be prepared to face suffering? Because this world is still full of suffering and God still is reaching into it and sending his children there as agents of reconciliation and healing. The worst can become the best by the working of divine grace through God's obedient people. Crowns can be forged out of thorns.

13

GOD WITH US ALWAYS

If Only Someone Were by My Side!

> I know the things that happen, the loss and the loneliness and the pain. . . . But there's a mark on it now: as if Someone who knew that way Himself, because He had traveled it, had gone on before and left His sign; and all of it begins to make a little sense at last—gathered up, laughter and tears, into the life of God, with His arms around it!
>
> —Paul Scherer

Jesus said, "I will be with you to the end of the age" (Matt 28:20).

The very birth of Jesus started off badly. There was no room in the facilities of Bethlehem for the birth itself, and afterwards Herod heard of the birth, was threatened, and sent thugs to kill the new baby. The parents had to grab what little they had and rush off to Egypt for safety. Once Jesus had grown up, things were no better. His life was a series of crises that finally ended in a public execution. The whole thing appears to have been a general disaster—or was it?

The New Testament claims that the end result of the troubled life of Jesus was God's wonderful victory on behalf of our sin and suffering in this tortured world. That judgment is an odd turn of events, to say the least. How could such an almost inconceivable thing possibly be true?

The dramatic news broadcast by the early church doesn't hide any of the tortured life and gruesome death of Jesus. Despite that, the news was good, really good. Inspired disciples proclaimed far and wide that God had been with us on behalf of all our troubles. Salvation had come, not only in spite of but actually *because of* the sufferings of Jesus. Amazing, especially if true.

We have come a long way to this point in exploring the jagged journey of the followers of the crucified Jesus. Faith seeks to find its way in the midst of suffering and in the wake of Jesus. We have faced the problem head on. Given the persistence of evil, can God even be, or at least be all-powerful and truly good? Could it be that, because of the evil now in the creation, God suffers too? We have insisted that our hurting isn't automatically our fault, at least not all of it. Something has gone wrong on a scale bigger than us and our own sinning. The result brought tears to the eyes of Jesus, an expression of the grieving heart of a loving God.

> Sometimes we only plant and others water; we weed and others harvest. Maybe the work is for us and the glory for our children or their children.

Despite the difficulty, we have determined to trudge down the rocky and slippery pathway of faith's search for understanding and support and survival. We fragile humans hurt and sometimes even despair, but we need not give up. We have learned that it's wise to doubt even some of our own doubts. We have realized that the darkest night has the bright stars and that God is at work for good whatever the darkness. We have come to realize that the worst of trials can train us for a higher Christ-likeness. Even thorns can be fashioned into a crown.

The proper pathway of faith in Jesus was pioneered by Paul (2 Cor 12:8-9-10). He faced a world of negatives and at first said, "Take it away!" (vs. 8). Then he learned that God's grace could be sufficient (vs. 9). Finally, he was inspired to rejoice in the fact that, when placed in God's hands, our human weakness can be strength that survives and even thrives in all things (vs. 10). That's the *8-9-10* pathway down the jagged journey of faith. The downward way of suffering can lead upward and finally to a fully healed home.

Now we gaze directly into the growing light ahead. It can happen—our very weakness can become our newest and greatest strength. The growing darkness can yield to a quietly invading and most welcome light. The cross of Jesus, torture instrument of the worst kind, somehow can be transformed into hope for the best, our salvation now and our total healing forever.

The big question remains, nonetheless. How can we make it, finish this jagged journey, even manage to sing on our way home? It may be a long and difficult trip, but it's been completed by many and can be managed by us, as long as we stay *in Christ* who is the Way.

Here's an important key to success, especially when suffering. Know that you are not alone. Whatever the struggle, *God is in it with you*. God is always by your side! Even if the path of the faith journey leads into the shadowy valley of death, the Shepherd is there and about to raise the curtain on a bright new future, the heights of eternal glory!

Saturday's a Hard Day

The pain goes deep when a life goal is blocked, especially when the goal was for the good of God's people. You said "yes" to what you thought was good, and God's simple and shocking answer was a flat "no." Reports a friend, "I wanted to be a minister but my church never made a place for me—maybe just because I was a woman." Says another, "I wanted to nurture a child of my own into life and faith, but the doctor said my body couldn't conceive." A man admits, "She was the love of my life. Just before our wedding a man we had never met had too much to drink, took the wheel himself, and my love and future went away in the crash."

People, good people, Christian people are frustrated and die all the time, having not received the fullness of their dreams. We sometimes pass it off with, "That's life!" It's the way things go in this world. Our faith journey inevitably is jagged, sometimes confusing, frequently disappointing. But is it still possible?

How heartbreaking can be the shock and the mystery of frustration and injustice. It's a suffering that can't be covered with a bandage or fixed with a pill. If there's a reason why things sometimes don't work out, despite our best efforts and sincerest prayers, it's beyond our meager understanding, and it's not just we who experience this. It's been common among God's people from the beginning.

Check the biblical record. Moses felt frustration and loss, as did Jeremiah, Paul, and even Jesus. The Lord did the Father's will perfectly and yet found himself reaching out to God with his humanity, so hoping that the cross might be avoided. He yielded willingly to its apparent necessity, but longed for it to be otherwise. Some things can't be avoided.

David surely knew deep frustration. He wanted to build a great house for God. It was not to be. His response? He determined to resource the coming generation so that it might do what he couldn't. He turned pain and frustration into planning and praise, laying foundations on which others could build. The thorns were melted and later would be reshaped into a crown. Pain today was yielding to possibilities for tomorrow. Sometimes we only plant and others water; we weed and finally others harvest. Maybe the work is for us and the glory for our children or their children. If that's the case, so be it—and the God of all generations is to be praised!

Some of the psalms attributed to David are full of pain. Injustice reigns and hope is lost behind black clouds. A remarkable thing about Israel is that it didn't deny the darkness but took it right into its religious life. Psalm 137, for instance, cries out in pain.[135] Life, even the life of faith, can be an arena of terror, a ragged place, a jagged journey, a series of empty and waiting Saturdays. If God indeed is always with us on this journey, there certainly are times when evidence is hard to find. No matter. Face facts and journey on.

One Saturday was an especially hard day for the first disciples of Jesus. Their Master had been humiliated, shamed, beaten, and dragged to that awful cross. Now he was dead and apparently they would be without him from now on. Yes, he had hinted at some great good yet to come, maybe a resurrection? But something amazing like that hadn't happened yet, and probably never would. The ugly world had won. Suffering reigned supreme.

It was the Saturday before Easter Sunday, waiting and hoping time, frustration and fear time, a terrible alone time. In that difficult vacuum when it's hard to breath and just survive, the Bible speaks. The news is this: "Whereas it was in your heart to build, you did well" (1 Kgs 8:17–19). When and even whether you see your desire fulfilled is not the only thing, maybe not the most important thing. God is faithful across the generations, among the passing of empires, during and beyond all Saturdays. Do your little part well in the present and God will care for the tomorrows.

Saturday is here. Don't despair. Sunday is surely coming. God is in the resurrection business. We who believe are not called to be "successful," only faithful. Said Paul, "I have not attained, but I still press toward the mark" (Phil 3:14). Pain or not, press on! Anticipated accomplishments or not, pray and praise on! Jesus would gladly echo the advice of a modern poet: "March on. Do not tarry. To go forward is to move toward perfection. March on and fear not the thorns or the sharp stones on life's path."[136]

The writer to the Hebrews tells us what makes possible a moving on without fear: "Keep running the race with patience, *looking to Jesus*" (12:2). Jesus is our pioneer and great resource for managing the rugged race. He overcame everything and now sits at the right hand of the Father. Keep looking to him, not to your present frustration and suffering, not to the thorns and sharp stones on the path. Remain in right relationship with Jesus and your future is secure. Why? *Because Jesus is the future!*

By the way, Sunday did come for those first disciples—Easter resurrection! A glorious Sunday is always on God's horizon. Therefore, with all the pioneers of our faith cheering us on, we are to "strip down, start running—and never quit!" Charge forward on the jagged journey remembering that "others have suffered far worse than you, to say nothing of what Jesus went through" (Heb 12:1-4). According to 1 Peter 5, "It's the same with Christians all over the world. . . . The suffering won't last forever. It won't be long before this generous God who has great plans for us in Christ—eternal and glorious plans they are!—will have you put together and on your feet for good. He gets the last word; yes, he does."

> Whatever dangers we currently face, Jesus remains the everlasting, nourishing, and comforting One who will outlast it all and remains by our sides.

Those of us who live for Jesus, and sometimes suffer and die for him, are blessed with the availability of this robust hope. Whatever happens in the meantime, one day we will rise with the Master into eternal bliss. According to John's great vision at the Bible's end, "Never again will they hunger; never again will they thirst. The sun will not beat down on them, nor any scorching heat. For the Lamb at the center of the throne will be their shepherd; he will lead them to springs of living water. And God will wipe away every tear from their eyes." (Rev. 7:16-17)

To whom was John writing this book of Revelation? It was to Christians suffering terrible things. It probably was written near the end of the first century when the Roman emperor Domitian was conducting large-scale persecutions of Jesus people. Some had their homes plundered while some were sent into the arena in Rome to be torn apart by wild beasts. And what did John give them so they could face it all? It was the ultimate hope. A new world was coming one day and already was being seen because Jesus had come. Soon things would be very different. Even death could be survived, and with joy! In the big picture, given the resurrection of Jesus, death in fact is already dead!

Pastor Donald Grey Barnhouse suffered his wife's death when his daughter was still a child. He tried to help himself and the little girl process this tragic loss. Once, when they were driving on a busy highway, a huge moving van passed them. As it passed, the shadow of the truck swept over the car. The minister shared a sudden thought with the girl. "Would you rather be run over by a truck or by its shadow?" The obvious reply, "By the shadow of course. That can't hurt us at all." Exactly. Even the shadow of suffering and the shroud of death are about to pass by, but they have no enduring substance. Soon they will be off the scene and replaced with a blaze of eternal light!

That shadow-only illustration brought a beautiful bottom line to the conversation between Barnhouse and his daughter. Concluded the pastor-father, "If the truck doesn't hit you, but only its shadow, then you're fine. Well, it was only the shadow of death that went over your mother. She's actually alive—more alive than we are. And that's because two thousand years ago the real truck of death hit Jesus. And because death crushed Jesus, and we believe in him, now the only thing that can come over us is the shadow of death, and the shadow of death is but our entrance into glory."[137] Today may be Saturday, but God's Sunday is just around the corner. Believe and move on.

Leaving the Upper Room

There's an amazing scene recalled in chapter 26 of Matthew's gospel. In a world of hate and raw power about to collapse on them and crucify their Master, the little group of Jesus' disciples huddled in an out-of-the-way place in Jerusalem to celebrate Passover. They were determined to honor an ancient tradition the best they could despite their ominous circumstances. Might God protect them and Jesus as he once did their ancestors of old? They surely needed "passed over" as evil surrounded them. Could they survive what seemed an impending and inescapable doom?

That place, an upper room, became a temporary sanctuary of peace and safety. These disciples soon heard this from the Master. "Let not your hearts be troubled." Despite what was very near, Jesus told them, "I will not leave you comfortless." His voice, although soft and gentle, sounded louder than the marching legions of mighty Rome outside, more penetrating than the ugly nails about to plunge into his innocent flesh, hanging him in the blistering sun to die a horrific death. Peace and safety? Hardly. Not for long. Horror was standing just outside.

That was then. Now, after the passing of so much time since that fateful day, we can see the larger picture that the disciples could not. Beyond the cross of Jesus would come a resurrection that was beyond belief. We now know that the hope announced in that little room of brief refuge has outlasted the empire crouched outside then, and all others that have arisen and threatened since. What was said soothingly by Jesus long ago was destined to endure to the last syllable of recorded time, ours included, no matter what. "Let not your hearts be troubled." "I will not leave you comfortless."

Earlier, Jesus had said this. "Abide in me and I abide in you." He had put this abiding graphically. "I am the true vine and my Father is the husbandman." Words of comfort. Promises of presence. Hope from Jesus. Whatever dangers we currently face as disciples of this eternal Master, whatever upper room we are huddled in seeking a little safety, Jesus remains the ever-living and nourishing and comforting One. He will outlast it all and he chooses to remain right by our sides.

Hearing again these words of Jesus, we can understand what Matthew Arnold once reported. He described a walk he took on a sweltering summer day through the vile slums of East London:

> I met a preacher there I knew, and said:
> "Ill and overworked, how fare you in this scene?"
> "Bravely!" said he, "for I of late have been
> Much cheer'd with thoughts of Christ,
> *The living bread."*

Much cheered in a vile slum? Thoughts of the presence of Christ moved the preacher and can move us beyond circumstance to hope. Despite suffering, we can sense a coming joy. Nourishment comes no matter what. It's enabled by a living bread that ever lives and nourishes.

Wise perspective often appears only with the aid of passing time. It was that way in the lives of David, Paul, and an endless parade of the children of God. For instance, the Bible reports that the history of the beloved King David was told fully by the chronicler, including "the times through which he and Israel and the surrounding kingdoms passed" (1 Chr 29:30). David couldn't see the fullness of the work of God in his life, not as a whole and not while immersed in the immediacy of his life's many happenings. God could, and now we can.

Our passing times are sometimes experienced as troubled days flooding over us like a surging surf, wave after wave smashing on us like a helpless rock. Time comes at us like "an ever-rolling stream" that wears us down and threatens finally to take away all its sons and daughters. Who or what remains in the midst of all our experiences? Who decides what's left when it's over? What can we see when looking back across the whole of our lives? Has the bad destroyed the good, or has the good persistently infused the bad and finally triumphed?

In David's case, there was a shepherd boy, prince, outlaw, guerrilla leader, king, sinner, penitent, and saint—all in one life! Somehow, throughout this jagged journey, David's destiny had been cradled in the hands of God. Even in the things that went desperately wrong, eventually it could be seen that the waves pounding on this life somehow were made to serve God's ultimate purpose. In the end, God rules the waves. As Paul would report later, the dramatic and often negative events in his missionary career had "turned to the furtherance of the gospel" (Phil 1:12).

We hear an encouraging echo from a beleaguered but still victorious apostle of Jesus. In the final two verses of the New Testament, John reports this. Jesus, who testifies to all these things, says *to you and me*:

> "I'm on my way! I'll be there soon!"
> Yes! Come, Master Jesus!
> The grace of the Master Jesus be with all of you.
> Oh, Yes!"[138]

That's what the whole life of faith teaches us. We have a triple hope. First, *God is with us in it all.* Second, *God will be here soon to relieve all suffering and right all wrongs.* Even when seeming to be the most absent, and when we are the most anxious and afraid, there arrives the third. *God's coming is sure, unstoppable, and almost here.*

By contrast, reading Psalm 88 can be disturbing indeed, but it's also part of the real life of faith. A child of God is overheard saying, "Abandoned as already dead, one more body in a stack of corpses.... You've dropped me into a bottomless pit." What's a psalm like that doing in the Bible? Just this. The Bible speaks to all of life, to all dimensions of the jagged journey, not just to the good things and good times. Even when acknowledging the bad times, we are being prepared for the glory soon to come.

The jagged journey of Christian faith can have its dark moments, and they shouldn't be denied. But there's more than that. The cry of pain, even in the darkest of the psalms, is not one of total depression and hopelessness. It's a prayer that still has the great Someone to whom we can speak. Even in the pit, God is and God hears.

The ever-with-us God is known only to the spiritually mature. God comes to be known more and more even while continuing to be the great mystery. Faith knows that it doesn't have all insights and answers. The *why* of this or the *how* of that or the *when* of the other thing is often out of reach. Can we find rest and hope in the midst of such admitted ignorance?

The hope we need so desperately need not come from our knowing all the *whys* or *hows* or *whens* that trouble our lives in this world. Deep rest and abiding hope and rich joy come only from the persistent presence of *Who*. What has come within our reach is assurance that *Someone* is there, a gracious and eternal Someone, always there and really there for us. Joseph and Mary named him Jesus, and we must claim him as LORD.

Over time, as we mature in faith and gain in Christ-likeness, God becomes less the *object* of our believing and more the present and comforting *source* of our wonder! In that immensity, in that righted relationship is our peace. In that intimacy is our comfort. This is only how we can believe that "the sufferings of this present time are not worth comparing with the glory about to be revealed in us" (Rom 8:18).

Battle of Land and Sea

A great insight hit him when he was wandering aimlessly on an isolated New Zealand seashore. Pastor Boreham saw miles and miles of wreckage, the remains of a titanic struggle of the ages. The combatants? The sea and the land. Clearly the waters had won even though they were soft and fluid and the land was composed of huge and seemingly solid rock cliffs.

Pondered the pastor, "the land makes no impression on the sea, but the sea grinds the land to powder." This is also seen in Arizona by gazing at the Grand Canyon. One river, millions of years, and what is left from the flowing of the water? A huge crevice in the earth's surface. The lesson? "It is the triumph of the eternal."[139] Simple water eventually conquering towering cliffs of stone. It's an unlikely, stunning, and spiritually reassuring scene.

A carpenter coming from tiny Nazareth with soft words of love, a gentle flowing of the water of life, a message poised to conquer the world, an unlikely scenario. Can the "weak" things of this world finally overcome the mighty forces of evil? Yes, they surely can. The work of God will prevail in its own time and way. That's the long view, the big picture. Psalm 3 presents a defiant faith fixed on this big picture. Enemies were on every hand, but salvation belongs to God. The triumph of God is inevitable despite all present appearances. Stone will become dust and the sea will prevail.

Shadrach, Meshach, and Abednego were in a helpless position. Soon they would be burned alive for not bowing to a foreign idol. Recant? Why not? After all, God was not seeming to help them in this urgent time of need. Even so, their faith didn't falter. God will deliver, they were sure, *but if not* . . . (Dan 3:17-18). If God didn't deliver from the fire, they were determined to remain true despite the momentary suffering. They were convinced of the larger picture, the eventual outcome.

Like Job, their attitude was one of invincible worship—"though He slay me, yet will I trust Him" (Job 13:15). God stands in and beyond the fire. Now or later, one way or another, the mills of God will grind to dust all passing pretenders to the divine throne. By the way, back to Shadrach, Meshach, and Abednego in that horrid fire ordered by the king, there appeared a mysterious fourth man who "looked like a son of the gods" (3:25). We who are faithful are never left alone!

> I know loss, loneliness, and pain. But Someone has left His sign, and it begins to make a little sense at last—gathered up, laughter and tears, into the life of God, with His arms around it!
>
> —*Paul Scherer*

Matthew tells of an awful storm in which Jesus came walking on the waves and leveled them into peaceful ripples (Matt 8:23-27). When barely surviving in the midst of the storm, how easy it is to see only the waves and not the Master. But "the man who has found God is not the hopeless slave of circumstances and events. His true life is not at the mercy of the ravages of time. The times go over him: the man *remains*."[140] God is always by the side of the faithful.

The suffering wave of death is the last to go over us, but even that has no real impact. Knowing the life of God *now* reduces death to no more than a transition into knowing the same life of God *then* and *always*. The smashing wave of this life's ending splashes wildly in all directions and then is no more. The rock that is God is unharmed and immortal. That which is born of the Spirit is Spirit and lives forever. The house built on high ground withstands all storms (Matt 7:24–27).

Here's the way to go through difficulty when it refuses to go away. Fix your gaze on the bigger picture. Paul put it plainly to the troubled Corinthian church. "Since God has so generously let us in on what he is doing [the big picture], we're not about to throw up our hands and walk off the job just because we run into occasional hard times" (2 Cor 4:1).

To see the bigger picture, something is necessary. According to Jesus, "You're blessed when you get your inside world—your mind and heart—put right. Then you can see God in the outside world" (Matt 5:8). Repent, believe, be renewed, and have your eyes opened. A battle of land and sea is in progress. The rocky land is doomed. The future belongs to God and all who are in right relationship with the framer of worlds, past and future.

The King Comes!

The big-picture reality comes through the wonderful Greek word *parousia*. The most common meaning is "presence" or "arrival." Paul was comforted by the "arrival" of Titus (2 Cor 7:6). In Hellenistic use well known to many early Christians, *parousia* referred to the arrival of a visiting king or governor. This prominent coming often called for new taxes to pay for a special gift for the king and possibly the striking of a new coin in his honor.

In the New Testament, the word has specific reference to the "second coming" of Jesus, king of the universe (2 Pet 1:16, etc.). Such a grand event has requirements for us. Life must be preserved blameless and preparations made (1 Thess 3:13; 5.23; 1 John 2:28). Patience is required since suffering still goes on and all will not be righted until that judgment day finally arrives (Jas 5:7–8). A Christian can endure anything in the meantime because it's already known that *the King is coming!* The emptiness and anxiety experienced in suffering and waiting can be replaced by the fullness of expectancy of the coming Presence.

A blind person, it once was said, can always spot a poor congregation. How? He or she hears the preacher quoting, "Where two or three are gathered together in My name, there am I in the midst of them." That usually means that most of the pews are empty. But this text is not so much about missing worshippers. "It is not an apology for human absence. It is a triumphant proclamation of the divine presence!"[141]

A favorite gospel song of Martin Luther King Jr. is said to have been "Take my Hand, Precious Lord." In the midst of great trouble, it affirms and calls on the great Presence:

> Precious Lord, take my hand
> Lead me on, let me stand,
> I'm tired, I'm weak, I'm lone;
> Through the storm, through the night
> Lead me on to the light,
> Take my hand, precious Lord, lead me home.[142]

We surely know the tiredness and weakness and loneliness. We also can know the hand of the precious Lord.

An aging cowboy knew that precious divine hand and sensed that his own days were numbered. For what did he pray when in the falling dusk he would get his final call? "Above all else, the happiest trail would be for You [God] to say to me, 'Let's ride, My Friend!'" The King is coming and prepared to join us in the final stage of our journey home. The jagged journey will melt into a joyous homecoming.

What's the big picture that only the spiritually mature can see? Just this. "The Lord God omnipotent reigneth!" (Rev 19:6). The central fact of life for Jesus wasn't home, family, work, or current safety and comfort. All of these had meaning for him, but he knew that they were passing things. He could see that Caiaphas, Pilate, Herod, Caesar, and all the rest were little more than dust beneath the chariot wheels of time.

Seeing the present this way leads to a grand conclusion. "The symphony God is composing includes minor chords, dissonance, and tiresome fugal passages. But those of us who follow his conducting through early movements will, with renewed strength, someday burst into song."[143]

Paul began his great letter to the Colossians with this wonderful testimony. He had been sent on a special mission as part of God's master plan. When we look at the Son, Jesus, he announces, "we see God's original purpose in everything created." The apostle summarizes God's big plan this way: "Christ is in you, so therefore you can look forward to sharing in God's glory." Focus should never be on momentary distractions, sufferings of today or worries about what might be tomorrow. It must be on the Christ who holds everything together, now and for all eternity.

As we grope about in the darkness of life's difficulties, sometimes passing through the deepest of waters or walking through the hottest of fire, the promise of Isaiah 43:1–2 holds true: "Do not fear, for I have redeemed you; I have called you by name, you are mine. When you pass through the waters, I will be with you; and through the rivers, they shall not overwhelm you; when you walk through fire you shall not be burned, and the flame shall not consume you." To this there is only one appropriate response. "Amen, so be it, LORD!"

Notes

1. Harold S. Kushner, *When Bad Things Happen To Good People* (New York: Schocken, 1981; Anchor, 2004).
2. Philip R. Meadows, "Reasonable Extremists: Christian Freedom in a Post-Christendom Society." Plenary address to the Wesleyan Theological Society, Wilmore, KY, March, 2017.
3. George MacDonald, *Unspoken Sermons, First Series*, as quoted by C. S. Lewis, *The Problem of Pain* (New York: MacMillan, 1940), frontpiece.
4. Eugene H. Peterson, *The Pastor: A Memoir* (Kindle ed., New York: HarperCollins, 2011), 7. Italics added.
5. This program of Chicago Theological Seminary was innovative and socially daring. Actually, I met the requirement by traveling in the Middle East and touring new refugee camps, just as heartbreaking to view but less threatening personally.
6. James Stewart, *The Strong Name* (New York: Charles Scribner's Sons, 1941), 125–68.
7. Elizabeth Kübler-Ross, *On Grief and Grieving: Finding the Meaning of Grief through the Five Stages of Loss* (New York: Scribner, 2005).
8. Larry Walkemeyer, *A Good Walk Home: A Parable on Living and Dying Well* (Glendora, CA: Aldersgate, 2013), preface.
9. C. S. Lewis, *The Problem of Pain* (San Francisco: HarperSanFrancisco, 1940), 91.
10. Douglas John Hall, *God & Human Suffering* (Minneapolis: Augsburg, 1986), 21.

NOTES

11. David Kinnaman, *You Lost Me: Why Young Christians are Leaving Church . . . and Rethinking Faith* (Grand Rapids: Baker, 2011), 219.

12. Jerry Bridges, *Trusting God* (Colorado Springs, CO: NavPress, 1988; Kindle ed. 2008).

13. George A. Buttrick, *God, Pain, and Evil* (Nashville: Abingdon, 1966), 33.

14. Walter Brueggemann, *The Message of the Psalms* (Minneapolis: Augsburg, 1984).

15. In my own autobiography I put this O-D-R path in graphic form and illustrate it with my personal life journey (*A Pilgrim's Progress*, Emeth and Anderson University Presses, 2nd ed., Lexington, KY, and Anderson, IN: 2013), Appendix G.

16. Brueggemann, *The Message of the Psalms*, 19, 23.

17. Barry L. Callen, *God As Loving Grace* (Nappanee, IN: Evangel, 1996), 121. Reprint, Wipf & Stock, 2018.

18. Barry L. Callen, *Heart of the Matter* (Lexington, KY: Emeth, 2016), 32–33.

19. Barry L. Callen, *Clark H. Pinnock: Journey Toward Renewal* (Nappanee, IN: Evangel, 2000).

20. Bridges, *Trusting God*.

21. Hall, *God & Human Suffering*, 98, 104–105.

22. Kushner, *When Bad Things Happen To Good People*, 81, 114, 127, 134, 140.

23. Leslie D. Weatherhead, *Salute to a Sufferer* (Nashville: Abingdon, 1962), in the closing paragraphs.

24. Barry L. Callen, *Bible Stories for Strong Stomachs* (Eugene, OR: Cascade, 2017), 92–93.

25. Philip Yancey, *Where Is God When It Hurts?* (Kindle ed., Grand Rapids: Zondervan, 1990).

26. Hall, *God & Human Suffering*, 158.

27. Karl Rahner, "Easter: A Faith that Loves the Earth," in *The Great Church Year*, ed. A. Raffelt (New York: Crossroad, 1994), 196.

28. Hall, *God & Human Suffering*, 166–67.
29. Buttrick, *God, Pain, and Evil*, 125.
30. John Calvin, *Institutes* 1.18.1.
31. Leslie D. Weatherhead, *The Will of God* (New York: Abingdon, 1944).
32. "Universalism" is the view that all humanity will be saved eventually. While this view is in accord with God's original will, the Bible strongly suggests that such an ideal outcome will not be the case. The ultimate evil is that many will continue to resist God's loving overtures and God finally will allow their choices to be permanent.
33. Peterson, *A Pastor*, 230. Italics added.
34. Lewis, *The Problem of Pain*, 16.
35. Evelyn Underhill, *Mysticism* (New York: Doubleday, 1990), 20.
36. See the Richard Michael Riss, "The Latter Rain Movement of 1948 and the Mid-Twentith Century Evangelical Awakening." PhD diss., Drew University, 2007.
37. William Shakespeare, *Macbeth*, Act 4, Scene 3.
38. See chapter 1 in Callen, *Bible Stories for Strong Stomachs*.
39. Lewis, *The Problem of Pain*, 132.
40. Ibid., 3.
41. Lewis, *Surprised by Joy* (United Kingdom: Geoffrey Bles, 1955).
42. One recent attempt to explore this difficult territory is Thomas Jay Oord, *The Uncontrolling Love of God: An Open and Relational Account of Providence* (Downers Grove, IL: InterVarsity, 2015).
43. This judgment is argued convincingly by Don Thorsen, *Calvin Vs Wesley: Bringing Belief in Line with Practice* (Nashville: Abingdon, 2013). He says, for instance, "Wesley provides a better understanding of Christianity and the Christian life in *practice* than Calvin does in *theory*" (xiv).
44. James Stewart, *Walking with God* (Vancouver, BC: Regent College Publishing, 2006), 25–27.
45. See the book by Oord, *The Uncontrolling Love of God*, 94.

46. See Barry L. Callen and Hubert P. Harriman, *Color Me Holy* (Glendora, CA: Aldersgate, 2013).
47. Barry L. Callen, *In Deep Water* (Lexington, KY: Emeth, 2009), 217, 131.
48. Elie Wiesel, *Night* (New York: Bantam, 1982), 62.
49. Corrie Ten Boom, from the movie *The Hiding Place* (1975).
50. See Bertrand Russell, *Why I Am Not a Christian and Other Essays on Religion and Related Subjects* (New York: Simon & Schuster, 1957).
51. For seven Bible stories that highlight the surprises of who God is and how God works, see Callen, *Bible Stories for Strong Stomachs*, chapters 8–14.
52. *A Preacher's Guide to Lectionary Sermon Series: Thematic Plans for Years A, B, C* (Kindle ed., Louisville: Westminster John Knox, 2016), 451–57.
53. Timothy Keller, *Walking with God through Pain and Suffering* (Kindle ed., New York: Penguin, 2013), 120.
54. See Barry L. Callen, *Caught Between Truths: The Central Paradoxes of Christian Faith* (Lexington, KY: Emeth, 2007).
55. Walter Brueggemann, *An Unsettling God: The Heart of the Hebrew Bible* (Minneapolis: Fortress, 2009), xii.
56. Theodore Jennings Jr., *Loyalty to God* (Nashville: Abingdon, 1992), 99.
57. Buttrick, *God, Pain, and Evil*, 55.
58. James D. Smart, *The Creed in Christian Teaching* (Louisville: Westminster, 1962), 129.
59. Max Lucado, *You'll Get Through This: Hope and Help for Your Turbulent Times* (Kindle ed., Nashville: Thomas Nelson, 2013), 7.
60. Clark H. Pinnock, *Most Moved Mover* (Grand Rapids: Baker Academic, 2001), 58.
61. See this amazing biblical story dramatized in Callen, *Bible Stories for Strong Stomachs*, 213ff.
62. Jürgen Moltmann, *The Crucified God* (London: SCM, 1973), 205.

63. Hall, *God & Human Suffering*, 158.

64. Nicholas P. Wolterstorff, *Lament for a Son* (Eerdmans, 1987), 90.

65. Hall, *God & Human Suffering*, 156.

66. Max Lucado, *God Came Near* (e-book ed., Nashville: Thomas Nelson, 1986).

67. Jürgen Moltmann, *The Crucified God* (40th anniversary ed., Minneapolis: Fortress, 2015), x.

68. Callen, *God As Loving Grace*, 75.

69. Randy Maddox, *Responsible Grace* (Nashville: Kingswood, 1994), 55. See Wesley in his New Testament notes on Romans 8:28 and in his sermon "The Great Assize."

70. Dietrich Bonhoeffer in *Cost of Discipleship* (first published in Munich, Germany by Chr. Kaiser Verlag, 1937).

71. Hall, *God & Human Suffering*, 183–84.

72. Thomas Collins, *Pathway to Our Hearts: A Simple Approach to Lectio Divina with the Sermon on the Mount* (Kindle ed., Notre Dame, IN: Ave Maria, 2011).

73. William Sloane Coffin, *Letters to a Young Doubter* (Louisville: Westminster John Knox, 2005), 107–9.

74. See Callen, *Caught Between Truths*.

75. Elizabeth A. Dreyer, "Suffering in Christian Life and Experience," in Richard W. Miller, ed., *Suffering and the Christian Life* (digital ed., Maryknoll, NY: Orbis, 2013).

76. Richard Dawkins, *River Out of Eden: A Darwinian View of Life* (New York: Basic, 1996), 132–33.

77. Buttrick, *God, Pain, and Evil*, 35, 37.

78. Keller, *Walking with God through Pain and Suffering*, 30.

79. Ibid., 31.

80. Barry L. Callen, *Beneath the Surface: Reclaiming the Old Testament for Today's Christian* (Lexington, KY: Emeth, 2012), 143.

81. Ranier Maria Rilke, *Sonnets to Orpheus II*, 29. Nurturingthegiftofseeking.org.

82. Henri Nouwen, *Spiritual Formation: Following the Movements of the Spirit* (Kindle ed., New York: HarperCollins, 2010).

83. Helmut Thielicke, *Nihilism: It's Origin and Nature—With a Christian Answer* (London: Routledge and Kegan Paul, 1961), 177.

84. R. B. Y. Scott, *The Way of Wisdom in the Old Testament* (New York: Macmillan, 1971), 141.

85. Brueggemann, *An Unsettling God*, 97.

86. Stewart, *Walking with God*, 183ff.

87. Malcolm Muggeridge, in *Homemade*, July, 1990. bible.org.

88. Max Lucado, *God Came Near* (iBook ed., Nashville: Thomas Nelson, 1986, 2004).

89. Hall, *God & Human Suffering*, 144.

90. Rohr, *Falling Upward: A Spirituality for the Two Halves of Life* (San Francisco: Jossey-Bass, 2011), 117.

91. Torah ends with Deuteronomy 34:4–12, the Prophets with Malachi 4:1–6, and the Writings with 2 Chronicles 36:22–23. The whole Bible ends with Revelation 22:1–7, sounding the same note of hope.

92. Dietrich Bonhoeffer, *Letters and Papers from Prison* (New York: Simon and Schuster, 1953).

93. Bruce Wilkinson, *The Prayer of Jabez: Breaking Through to the Blessed Life* (Sisters, OR: Multnomah, 2000).

94. Buttrick, *God, Pain, and Evil*, 187.

95. Henri Nouwen, *Spiritual Formation* (e-book, New York: HarperCollins, 2010).

96. Max Lucado, *You'll Get Through This* (Kindle ed., Nashville: Thomas Nelson, 2013), 53 of 224.

97. James Stewart, *The Wind of the Spirit* (Nashville: Abingdon, 1968), 113.

98. This story is told in Callen, *Bible Stories for Strong Stomachs*, chap. 22.

99. Billy Collins, "Flock," in *The Trouble with Poetry* (New York: Random House, 2005), 35.

100. Jürgen Moltmann, *A Broad Place: An Autobiography* (Minneapolis: Fortress, 2008), 30, 382.

101. My college alma mater, Geneva College, is associated with the Reformed Presbyterian Church. This small denomination with Scottish roots sings only the biblical psalms in worship. They provide a rich and wide-ranging spiritual experience.

102. Stewart, *Walking with God*, 53.

103. Ibid., 86.

104. Albert Schweitzer, *The Quest of the Historical Jesus* (London: Adam and Charles Black, 1911).

105. Barry L. Callen, *Catch Your Breath! Exhaling Death and Inhaling Life* (Glendora, CA: Aldersgate, 2014).

106. Clark H. Pinnock, *Flame of Love: A Theology of the Holy Spirit* (Downers Grove, IL: InterVarsity, 1996), 115.

107. Rohr, *Falling Upward*, 11, 20.

108. Carla Sunberg, *Reflecting the Image* (Beacon Hill Press of Kansas City, MO, 2015), 6, 57.

109. G. K. Chesterton, as quoted in C. Leonard Allen, *The Cruciform Church* (Abilene, TX: Abilene Christian University Press, 1990), 1.

110. Rohr, *Falling Upward*, 160.

111. As quoted by Philip Ryken, *Prayer of Our Lord* (Wheaton, IL: Crossway, 2002), 52–53.

112. For a full development of this truth, see Callen, *Caught Between Truths*.

113. Hymn "Take Time To Be Holy," William D. Longstaff, in *The United Methodist Hymnal*, 395.

114. Richard Rohr, *Falling Upward*, 132.

115. C. Leonard Allen, *The Cruciform Church*, 136–37.

116. Verse three of the hymn "How Firm a Foundation" based on 2 Timothy 2:19, Hebrews 13:5, and Isaiah 43:1–2.

NOTES

117. See Daniel S. Warner's biography, *It's God's Church!* by Barry L. Callen (Anderson, IN: Warner, 1995).

118. Barry L. Callen, *The Top Ten: Why Daniel S. Warner Is Still Relevant for You and Your Church* (Anderson, IN: Anderson University Press, 2015), 14.

119. Lewis, *The Problem of Pain*, 113.

120. Callen, *Catch Your Breath!*, 151.

121. F. W. Boreham, *Faces in the Fire* (Kindle ed., New York: Abingdon, n.d.).

122. Dale Oldham, *Giants Along My Path* (Anderson, IN: Warner, 1973).

123. Callen, *A Pilgrim's Progress*, 300–5.

124. Verse one of the Christian hymn "O Come, O Come, Emmanuel" dating back to the twelfth century in the original Latin text.

125. Part of verse one of the hymn by Charles Wesley titled "Love Divine, All Loves Excelling."

126. A famous book by Reinhold Niebuhr is titled *Moral Man and Immoral Society* (New York: Charles Scribner's Sons, 1932). He argues that the more formal the organization the less likely it is that it will (can) act in truly moral ways.

127. Billy Collins, "Reaper" in *The Trouble with Poetry* (New York: Random House, 2005), 52–53.

128. Frank Boreham, *The Luggage of Life* (Kindle ed., New York: Abingdon, 1918), 49ff.

129. Lewis, *The Problem of Pain*, 91.

130. Barry L. Callen, *Hope on the Horizon* (Pendleton, IN: Horizon International, 2010), 25.

131. Stewart, *Walking with God*, 118.

132. John Harris, *No Voice from the Hall* (London: John Murray, 1998).

133. See Roi Ottley's book *New World A-Coming* that won the Peabody and Life in America Awards (Boston: Houghton Mifflin, 1943).

134. David G. Buttrick, "Laughing with the Gospel," in Barry L. Callen, ed., *Sharing Heaven's Music: The Heart of Christian Preaching. Essays in Honor of James Earl Massey* (Nashville: Abingdon, 1995), 131.

135. For a brief but important study of such psalms of frustration and even anger, see Callen, *Bible Stories for Strong Stomachs*.

136. Khalil Gibran, accessed on BrainyQuote.com.

137. This story is told in many places, found here in Keller, *Walking with God through Pain and Suffering*, 317.

138. Revelation 22:20-21, *The Message* translation.

139. F. W. Boreham, "The Conquest of the Crags" in his *Faces in the Fire* (London: Epworth, 1933).

140. Stewart, *Walking with God*, 39.

141. Boreham, *The Luggage of Life*, 245.

142. Lyrics by Thomas A. Dorsey, made popular by Elvis Presley.

143. Yancey, *Where Is God When It Hurts?*

www.ingramcontent.com/pod-product-compliance
Lightning Source LLC
Chambersburg PA
CBHW030114170426
43198CB00009B/620